BEYOND
THE
DANCE

BEYOND
THE
DANCE

THOUGHTS FROM
A JOURNEY OF
SURRENDER

Yvonne Diez Peters

301 Lucien Way #415
Maitland, FL 32751
407.339.4217
www.xulonpress.com

Unless otherwise indicated, Scripture quotations taken from the New Living Translation. Copyright ©1996, 2004, 2007 by Tyndale House Foundation. Used by permission of Tyndale House Publishers, Inc.

Printed in the United States of America.

ISBN-13: 9781545608982

Table of Contents

INTRODUCTION

A JEWISH APHORISM, attributed to the Talmud states, "[Every man should] plant a tree, have a child, and write a book."[1] My husband and I planted a tree as part of our wedding ceremony. As a matter of fact, in lieu of flowers upon his death, several of my friends planted ten trees in the Jerusalem forest in his honor. I have not one, but two amazing children, and this is my first book. I think planting trees and birthing children are the easiest of the three.

The encouragement from friends, students, and peers to write this book has increased in the past eight years. Ultimately I knew it was incumbent upon me to just write it—scared! Don Newman, director of sales for Xulon Press, graciously helped demystify the process of getting started. Don said something in our initial meeting that sustained me when my self-critic was screaming awful things in my ear. "Yvonne," he said, "Remember the difference between an imperfect book that is read, and a perfect book that is never finished!" You are holding a less than perfect attempt in fulfilling the Talmudic trilogy.

The title of this book was suggested to me by my Brazilian friend and spiritual son, Robert Siqueira. Robert had encouraged me many times to write a book about my life experiences and ministry journey. In May of 2013 he sent me an email of condolence regarding Carl's passing. He signed off with this, a recounting of a dream he had. *"... and in the dream, I saw how God was doing, and performing a NEW TIME in your life. I woke up and I remembered how much I am thankful to God for everything I have learned from you, my dear pastor. I want to buy this book when the Lord permits you to write."*

I was in Brazil two years later and as we sat eating *acai* (an incredibly delicious frozen dessert) in a small cafe, he looked at me and said, "I have the name of the book: *Além da Dança,* translated to English, *Beyond the Dance.* Something about the title combined with his confident emphasis resonated with me.

As a medium of expression, dance drew me into an intimate communion with Jesus. Though I loved the craft, dance was not my identity. I had not been professionally trained before coming to faith in Christ. Dance was the language God chose to capture my heart and shape me into a worshipper, a Christ-follower, a disciple, and a teacher.

In the late 1970s dance, as an expression of worship, was practically nonexistent in the church. Biblically dance had been part of the worship experience throughout the ages, primarily through processions and celebration. In Psalm 42:4, King David laments, *"My heart is breaking as I remember how it used to be; I walked among the crowds of worshipers, leading a great procession to the house of God, singing for joy and giving thanks amid the sound of a great celebration."* There is also David's exuberant free dance of joy as he brought the Ark of the Covenant back to Jerusalem. Historically, dance has moved in and out of vogue as part of the worship liturgy. But in the context of the 1970s, it was neither embraced nor accepted by mainline denominations.

One reason I believe dance began to resurface in the church was in response to the "Jesus Movement" of the 1960s. The "Jesus Movement" captured a whole generation of young believers, many of whom were musicians and movement artists. Contemporary Christian music was given birth by these young pioneering musicians. Along with the musical artists were dancers who were coming into the church desiring to use dance as an expression of their worship. Many of us at that time created private space to worship God in dance in our living rooms, basements, and attics since there was no permission granted on Sunday mornings in the sanctuary. As pioneers in this worship expression, we would not meet each other until years later, but one thing we shared was our starting dates in the 1970s.

In 1983, I made my first pilgrimage to Jerusalem. Our church group toured the sites during the day. In the evenings we attended a global conference sponsored by the International Christian Embassy. In keeping the biblical mandate to celebrate the Feast of Tabernacles, the evening celebrations were extravagant demonstrations of worship. Three times a year the Israelites were to appear before God in Jerusalem. The Feast of Tabernacles was celebrated by rejoicing before the God of Israel for seven days. It was during one of the evening services I saw dancers participating in the worship service on stage. Prior to this 1983 experience my friend, Joanne Cecere, and I had been dancing locally in our church as a duo called "SONDANCE." As Joanne and I watched the dancers on stage, she leaned over to me and said, "Yvonne, we could do that." The whole experience was mesmerizing, surreal, and my level of unbelief so high, I replied, "No way, Joanne, no way!" When we arrived home from the tour, we began to explore the application process. We would have to raise our own funds to get there, and we would have to audition upon arrival. Through numerous fundraisers, we managed to get the needed money together, and we both passed the audition. What had seemed an impossibility became a reality. In the fall of 1984, I was dancing as a company member in Jerusalem, the City of the Great King.

Like the disciples who were originally sent from Jerusalem, the dance ministry was christened and international doors for ministry were opened. From 1984 to 2010 (with the exception of two years), I would spend four to six weeks out of my year in Jerusalem. In the beginning of my tenure with the International Christian Embassy, I was a member of the dance company, led by Randall Bane and Valerie Henry. For several years the three of us went on to tour the USA as "The Tabernacle Dance Company." In the early 1990s I became the company manager and one of the choreographers for the annual celebration. In 2001, one week after the events of September 11th, I became the dance director, and worked with life-long friend, worship leader, and artistic director Chuck King. During my years working with Chuck, we toured many cities internationally. We brought to their people the worship arts and the message of standing in support with Israel as Christian friends who honored a covenant with their same God. Out of these connections came many invitations to pioneer the art of dance as an expression of worship and to direct conferences in churches around the world. It has been an honor to serve God in the Philippines, South Africa, Nigeria, Brazil, the Russian Federation, the Baltic States, the Caribbean, and throughout Europe. In 2010 I retired as the dance company director from the International Christian Embassy Jerusalem.

In the introduction to his book, *The Grand Weaver,* Ravi Zacharias tells a beautiful story of how the elaborate wedding saris of Varanasi, India, are made.[2] This northern city in India is famous for creating breathtaking, six-yard-long fabrics to drape around brides on their wedding day. Not only are the colored threads for these saris made with brilliant dyes, but real gold and silver threads are also woven into the fabric.

For someone visiting a shop, curious to find out how the saris are made, what they would essentially find is a father-and-son team. The father sits on an elevated platform selecting a handful of threads for the design that only exists in the father's mind. His son sits at a lower level on the floor. As the father gathers the threads in hand, he nods to the son who moves the shuttle from side to side. The process of creating a splendid and unique wedding sari begins with only the father knowing the beauty of the finished design and the son being obedient to the father's command, both father and son working the process through to completion. What an incredible metaphor of God's perfecting ways and design in our lives.

I believe God intervenes throughout our lives, speaking to us uniquely through the divine DNA He has placed in us. My journey as a missionary to foreign nations and as a leading pioneer to restore the art of dance as an expression of worship to God began as a child on 3019 East Louisiana Avenue in Tampa, Florida. Although I was not aware a design was being woven for my life, each individual thread would have a purpose in forging my heart for worship.

Many dance experiences frame the stories in the book you hold in your hands. But that is only the veneer of the telling. God used the language of dance to capture my heart as a worshipper. When I said "yes" to surrendering control and allowing the Master to direct my steps to the specifications of His design, treasures were delivered into my life. These treasures were the lessons learned, the depth of friendships formed from people of all ethnicities and nations of the world, and the destiny of a call and purpose for a lifetime of walking with Jesus.

Placed in God's purposed eternal continuum and seasoned with measures of both deep joy and adversity, these are the snapshots of a journey with a loving God who is intimately acquainted and involved with all our ways. He alone takes the threads of what has gone before, weaves them into our now, and fashions an eternal destiny to what lies "Beyond the Dance."

This book is dedicated to my late husband, Carl B (no period) Peters. Even with his given name, there was a slight deviation from the norm. That was certainly predictive of Carl! He was the better writer of the two of us and penned many poems, short stories, plays, and essays. He never published, and yet here I am dedicating my first book to him. How ironic!

Metaphorically, I see my life as a trilogy. The prequel represents my childhood and early adult years. It's the setup for understanding the main character. Meeting Carl and the next forty years is "the story!" The transformational power at work in my life, the evolving destiny, the incredible adventures with world-wide travel, friends, and ministry, the challenges of marriage and raising children, facing cancer head-on, death, widowhood—this is my personal story. Carl was the constant steady. He believed, encouraged, and loved me through the best and worst of myself, many times being personally inconvenienced. It is not an exaggeration to say I would not be who I am, nor would I have accomplished as many goals had it not been for Carl.

And so, Babe this book is dedicated to you. Your imprint watermarks each page. Thank you for a life well lived. Thank you for loving me.

The sequel to the trilogy? It's presently being written. I'll be sure to let you know when it's published!

ACKNOWLEDGMENTS

WRITING AN ACKNOWLEDGMENT mentally unleashes a litany of names and faces. How do I begin without sounding as if I'd just won an Academy Award? Please be released to turn the page when you tire of reading.

My family. My parents Bobby and Pilar Diez, who were unconditional constants all through my life. My sisters Diana and Debbie, who know all my secrets and love me still. My children Zana and Rob, the supreme accomplishments of my life. Scott and Laurie, the spouses of my children and other half of the gene pool gifting me with the most amazing grands on the planet. My grandchildren Jacob, Brogan, Andrew, Cayman, Dylan, and Rylan. I'd relive your parents' teenage years just to have you all in my life!

My friends, who are my family. You have opened your hearts and homes countless times. We have shared life authentically in many seasons. Many of your children and grandchildren are part of my life. I am enriched because of your love and care.

My pastors and mentors. Richard Brown, Steve and Loretta Thompson, George and Linda Brooks, Barry Perez, Jeff and Sherry Ghiotto, Bill and Eva Hoopes, Bob and Sharon Perry, Sam and Paulette Farina, Torry and Marlyn Gligora, Geraldo and Cleide Diaz, the late Dr. E. Charlotte Baker, Dr. Sam Sasser, and Dr. Fuchsia Pickett. You laid my foundation and shaped my ways.

My ministry and dance partners. Joanne Cecere, Romeo Bagunu, Randall Bane, Valerie Henry, Chuck King, Teresa Gardner, Father Alejandro Rodriquez, Joe Beynon, Jubilate Dance Company, and Daryse Osborne. Dearest friends, you influenced my life in unforgettable ways. I am forever grateful and indebted to you.

My editor. Diane Woods Towry, I owe tremendous gratitude to you for your willingness to plow through this manuscript countless times offering your editorial expertise and creative ideas for chapter transitions. You were an amazing "cheerleader" for this project! You, sweet friend, are a gift sent from heaven.

My photographer. Barry Lively, you worked magic taking photographs from decades' past and getting them to publishing standards. Thank you also for gifting me with my first grandson!

My book cover designer. Ismarily Velazquez, your artistry, your intercession, and your love has made deep inroads into my heart. Thank you for your obedience to follow hard after the Lord.

Praise for
"Beyond the Dance"

I met Yvonne Peters in 1993 at the Exaltation Dance Conference our church hosted. Our introduction was brief, but God continued to weave our journeys. We have shared friendship, ministry, family celebrations, and sorrows—*LIFE*. Through the years, she has continued teaching me things. Those who are around Yvonne are always learning if they will listen. *Beyond the Dance* is a learning opportunity for all who read it. Her writing style is so relational, you might feel like you are having coffee together. You will enjoy every page of this book, and Yvonne will teach you things if you will listen.

Daryse Osborne
Choreographer
Director of Charisma Centre for the Arts,
Columbus, Ohio
Worship Staff, Christian Assembly, Columbus, Ohio

Beyond the Dance is as delightful a read, as Yvonne Peters is a person. The passionate love for her Lord that has been so beautifully expressed through her artistic gift of dance is now available through the written word of her life's testimony. More than a personal testimony, it is a definitive statement that God is at work in all our lives, even before we come into this world, and the choices we make will certainly influence generations to come. Read it! Be inspired, be encouraged, and be challenged for God's workmanship to be revealed in your own life.

Teresa Gardner, D.W.S.
(Doctor of Worship Studies)
Director, Zion Center for Worship and the Arts
Director, The Resurrection Dance Ministry

Beyond the Dance is a "must read." God graciously set a beautiful, dancing pioneer in time to forge the way for shifting worship paradigms. Designed to bring life-changing encounters with the King of the Universe, the pages of this book are filled with revelation from a humble servant with a heart of worship whose sacrifice of love changed lives and changed nations.

Dr. Pamela Hardy (USA)
Set Free Ministries
Eagles International Training Institute

Yvonne Peters is one of the strongest women I have ever met. I first met her in 1988 when she was dancing on tour with Integrity's Hosanna music. I'll never forget because she came down off the stage and reached out, took me by the hand, and off we went, dancing God's praises through the aisles with anyone else who would join. That was only the beginning. Over the last thirty years I have watched her life, faith, and dance and experienced true friendship standing the test of time. Working alongside her, I learned she's the real thing. She lives what she believes, loves God and people, and through trials has proven to be one of the most tender, transparent, and tenacious women I know. I love her. I've learned from her. You will, too.

Anna L. Valle
Fitness and Dance Professional

1990. It was my first time in Israel, and I was going to join the Feast of Tabernacles International Dance Company. I was a little scared, but as soon as I joined the first dinner table at the YMCA restaurant in Jerusalem, guess whose was the first welcoming smile to be opened for me? Yvonne's.

Samuel Esteves (Portugal)

Coming into our Christian walk of faith within a year of one another, Yvonne and I walked our formative years together. We learned about trust, faith, and friendship. However, most importantly, we learned to love Jesus and share His love with others. Yvonne is one of the most courageous women I know. Her stories are truly inspiring, and they can bring tears, as well as laughter. Now we can share in her experiences as we journey with her beyond the dance.

Thank you, Yvonne

Joanne Cecere (USA)
Worship Arts Director for
Beit Tehila Congregation

We have had the great joy of being a small part of Yvonne's "story" for thirty years although for us small is not an appropriate description. She was the catalyst and glue that held together not only a dance ministry, but lifelong friendships marked with unconditional love. We are beyond grateful to have been woven together in the tapestry of stories found beyond the dance.

Jubilate Dance Company

Once Upon a Time . . .

"You watched me as I was being formed in utter seclusion, as I was woven together in the dark of the womb." Psalm 139:15

THE ENGLISH PHRASE, "Once upon a time," dates back as far as Chaucer's *Canterbury Tales*, published in 1385.[3] It is used as the opening sentence in many fairy tales and epic stories, suggesting a time when a story begins, but implying there is more to tell. I believe it is a proper opening for my story.

Once upon a time in the late 1800s, a woman named Ignacia Gutierrez Ramirez lived a troubled life in Zaragoza, Spain. What disturbed her greatly was the discovery her husband and the father of her three children had a secret life. He was married to another woman from another city. After meeting the "other woman" and comparing stories, Ignacia decided to leave her husband, take the children, relocate to Barcelona, and reestablish her life. Living in Barcelona as a hair dresser proved to be difficult. In time, she realized she could not provide for her three children—Pilar, age nine; Santiago, age seven; and Carmen, age six.

The children were gifted artistically and enjoyed singing and performing for pocket change on the streets. Ignacia knew of an esteemed children's theatrical company that performed around the world. This company trained and cared for the children entrusted to them. After difficult emotional wrestlings, she made the decision to release Santiago, Pilar, and Carmen into the care of the director in the hope of reuniting with the children in a few months. Sadly, the children never saw her again until adulthood.

It was through this experience the children were trained for a lifetime career in the theater, learning to dance, sing, and act for audiences including kings and queens throughout Europe, South America, Mexico, and Cuba. Ignacia Guitierrez Ramirez is my great-grandmother. Carmen Ramirez is my grandmother.

My paternal grandfather, Fernando De San Jose Diez, was born in Arroyo Santander, Spain in 1875. He immigrated to the United States when he was eleven years old. While details and stories flourished from the maternal side of my heritage, I only have one story from my father's side. But this one episode sheds light on what was to shape my journey.

DIVINE DESIGN

"You know when I sit down or stand up. You know my thoughts even when I'm far away." Psalm 139:2

TWO SIGNIFICANT MEMORIES from my childhood would prove to be strong indicators and prophetic markers for my future. The weaving of these threads would establish the foundation of the design upon which all future patterns would be set.

At six years of age I lived on 3019 East Louisiana Avenue in Tampa, Florida in a section of the city known as Belmont Heights. This area of town was a mixture of the remnants from a former rural Tampa and a struggling economic population now giving way to low-income housing. My family was part of the populace giving way to lower incomes, but I never thought we were impoverished.

As a little girl I remember sitting on the sun-warmed cement steps of the front porch and watching people of color, both neighbors and strangers, walking past the house. Compassion stirred in my heart for people different than me. In the inner life of my six-year-old self I whispered prayers asking God "to bless everyone in the world." Though my universe was small, I sensed a vastness of life beyond my neighborhood and knew there had to be a God who governed over it all.

Overt practices of faith, prayer, and Bible reading were nonexistent in my home. My mother was a professing Catholic, but we never went to mass. My father, influenced by his father, was agnostic. And yet as I sat on the stoop, the love of God moved my heart for people beyond my small sphere of life.

Tied to prayers for those unlike me, I experienced in my own home the first stirrings of society's injustices. Brought up in the South, my family hired black Americans who helped with household chores. Ethel, a large and nearly toothless woman, came to wash and iron clothes for us. My father, a cattle rancher, also had several black Americans who worked for him. While there was no hostile treatment of these hired workers, any meals they ate in our home were served on separate dishes. This seemed strange to me since everyone else who ate in our home was served on the maroon and chartreuse Melmac dishes in the cabinets. Ethel and the other worker's dishes, however, were stored under the kitchen sink, an unclean space in our home. These dishes were used to feed the hunting dogs my father kept in the back yard. Though not certain I want to introduce the possibility these dishes were washed after feeding the dogs, and before being used to serve Ethel and my father's workers, I sincerely hope so! Clean or unclean dishes, in my six-year-old mind this situation felt unkind and unjust toward human beings different only in color.

There is a second poignant memory which shaped and marked my life—visits to my aunt's house. My beloved Aunt Leila's home was within walking distance from my home. In my childhood estimation her home seemed palatial. My father was raised in this homestead with his fourteen brothers and sisters. The most amazing—and my favorite— part of the house was the living room. It was carpeted and had a piano. My home had no carpeting and the glue that held the wallpaper to the walls was drying up, causing it to peel and hang halfway down the wall. Why my mother never pulled it off or reglued the paper to the wall remains a mystery to me today. At any rate, Aunt Leila would allow me, if I was very careful, to play by myself in the parlor. She also played the piano and on several occasions I had listened to her play "I Believe" by Frankie Laine. I memorized the lyrics. My favorite line went like this: *"I believe for every drop of rain that falls, a flower grows. I believe that somewhere in the darkest night, a candle glows, I believe for everyone who* *goes astray, someone will come to show the way, I believe, I believe.*⁵ I would "belt" the song, dancing to my own voice, and using her porcelain rose vase as a prop, I would lift it up to heaven as part of my dance. It was on one of these occasions I began to weep. I wept, because as I danced I sensed someone other than myself in the room. There is only one way I can describe how it felt. It was as if huge engulfing, warm, liquid waves of love were being poured over me. In that moment I sensed the tangible presence of God in the room. I felt the pleasure of this audience of One.

Here I was, a pudgy little girl grappling with prejudices I couldn't understand or articulate. Desiring for all the people of the world to be helped, I was unsettled by thoughts of man's injustice to man. Yet in my play time while I was dancing, the God of the entire universe revealed His love for me. Unfortunately, it would be another twenty-two years and some seriously bad choices before I even thought about these events again.

Rapunzel, Rapunzel, Let Down Your Hair

". . . and he will be called . . . Prince of Peace."
Isaiah 9:6

"Rapunzel" was my favorite fairy tale as a child. The Brothers Grimm adapted and published this story in 1812 as part of a children's collection.[7] The story is predated and influenced by an earlier story, *Petrosinella* by Giambattista Basile, published in 1634.

Captivating my imagination, even at a young age, the beauty of the relationship between Rapunzel and the prince stirred my heart for a longing to find my own prince someday. Rapunzel, for those who do not know the story, is raised by an evil enchantress who locks Rapunzel in a tower that has no entry either through doors or stairs. For the enchantress to reach her, Rapunzel must let down her plaited hair. Using her hair as a ladder the enchantress, named Dame Gothel, could then climb to the tower window. A prince riding in the forest discovers this scene. Waiting until Dame Gothel leaves, he calls to Rapunzel to let down her hair, and the two meet and fall in love. The wicked Gothel discovers the prince has been coming to Rapunzel. To thwart the lovers she cuts off Rapunzel's hair, banishes her into the forest, and then waits for the prince to return. The prince, unsuspectingly, climbs up the braided hair to be told he will never see Rapunzel again. In despair he leaps from the tower and falls into a thorn bush. The prince is blinded and left to wander in the forest. As fate and fairy tales would have it, Rapunzel and the prince find each other. Rapunzel weeps at finding her beloved to be blind. Cradling him in her arms, tears fall from her eyes, and his sight is miraculously restored.

Rapunzel's story fostered my search for a prince from kindergarten into adulthood. There was a short-lived boyfriend in first grade named Sammy, but it was junior high school where I met my first love. The relationship transitioned into my first year in high school. We even made the calendar couple for June. It was the perfect high school romance. I had found my prince—that is, until he was attracted to another princess! I was devastated. It would be another two years before I had my second boyfriend. My heart longed to be rescued from a deep-seated loneliness and desired a "forever" love. It was during these years I honed and perfected my skills at performance-based acceptance. I was an aspiring chameleon, changing colors to be whatever I thought might bring a prince my way. The liability of being a chameleon is losing your true self and "deceiving" any prince who might come your way.

My relationship with the second boyfriend lasted through college, and we married shortly before graduation. Soon we were four with the birth of a daughter and a son. The marriage did not last, but I am forever thankful for the gifts of Zana and Robby he gave me. They are precious treasures from this broken marriage. The longing for deep love, to be cherished, to be safe, to be rescued from a nagging loneliness continued to elude me. It is important for me to interject that while I was looking for a prince, I was no princess in waiting. I was broken and focused on desiring to be the "recipient" of love, and yet pitifully immature in knowing how to "give" love.

Following the divorce I began developing a new and invincible persona. This emerging woman was programed for recognition and hopefully a little fame. Clothes, shoes, hair, and a new exciting career with travel were my preoccupations. No more chameleon for me; I was fashioning myself into a strong image of my own liking. Thank God my mother and father were nearby and watched the children, offering stability for two very turbulent years. And my prince? I didn't think I needed one anymore. I was doing just fine on my own. I oversaw a new kingdom: mine. And I was at the center. In retrospect I am grateful life in my enchanted kingdom was short lived and I came to the end of myself quickly. While I knew I needed a rescue, the walls, gates, and moats surrounding my heart were impenetrable, even to a prince.

A chance meeting with a stranger and one date later in 1978 brought the beginning of the end to my hardened heart. Carl B Peters, a prince of a man, introduced me to a "genuine" prince—the Prince of Peace, Jesus the Christ. Meeting Carl began the process of recognizing my need for redemption, the need for a savior, the need of rescue by a Prince who could save me, forever! Like Rapunzel's prince, this Prince, who is also a King, proved His love through sacrifice. He loved me enough to die for me. And like Rapunzel I was overwhelmed to find this kind of unconditional sacrificial love. I wanted to give myself fully to loving the One who had so graciously loved me. I treasured Carl as a wonderful man: kind, sincere, thoughtful, and very handsome. But Jesus was one who plumbed the depths of my heart. The deep cries for healing, restoration, the release from shame, transformation, becoming a "new creation" in Christ—these desires could only be touched by the Prince of Peace. Only this Jesus could bring a healing balm to my heart's deepest ache and longing. Like Rapunzel's tears of love falling into the eyes of her beloved, my tears of repentance at His feet sealed a lasting love with my beloved Savior. The prequel of my trilogy was completed. My "story" was just beginning.

Gift from Carl: December 31, 1978

On lemon-stained and flat-iron-burned paper you created an invitation made to look like ancient parchment paper. It read, "You are cordially invited to help celebrate the King's birthday: Candlelight dinner for two. (Child-sitting service provided) R.S.V.P." So thankful I responded with a "yes!"

Wabi-Sabi and
Broken Hearts

*"He heals the broken-hearted and bandages
their wounds." Psalm 147:3*

MY FORMAL EDUCATION included graduating
from the University of South Florida with a BA in English
education. I spent two short years as a secondary teacher,
became very disillusioned with teaching, (I wanted to teach
Chaucer and ended up reading *Charlotte's Web* aloud just
to keep students in their seats!), and ultimately left the
education field altogether to join the corporate world for
a major film and camera company. While servicing one of
my company accounts during a normal work day, I met Carl
B Peters. A new pattern was about to be woven into God's
design for my life.

As I inventoried stock and filled out reports for orders
at the camera counter, I looked up and saw this cute twen-
ty-something, blond, blue-eyed man. I did not want to

engage with him I simply wanted to look. Like a child in a candy store I felt safe looking at the candy, but I did not want to buy any. But this guy was handsome! I continued with my paperwork and orders and stole another look. I was just getting ready to leave and stole a third glance, just one last time. He caught my gaze and spoke. Great! Now I had to talk to him. In doing so I discovered the reason he was there.

Seems he was an activities director at a local nursing home and was inquiring with the camera department manager regarding the possibility of her Girl's Scout troop making a visit to the nursing home. This was mid-December of 1978, and he was soliciting the troop for some caroling later that week. Unfortunately the camera manager could not make the date and declined the offer. To this day I can't believe what I did next. I offered to bring my children and some of their neighborhood friends to fill the gap. We arranged a time, and a few days later, I pulled in to the Tarpon Springs Nursing Home!

I met Carl B (no period, he would always say) Peters at a very difficult time in my life. Quite frankly I was a mess! I had come through a divorce and was raising two young children as a single working mother. I was self-medicating with drugs and alcohol. Not shockingly, I was also suffering from depression. He, of course, had no idea who he had invited into his world.

On that crisp December morning in the very first room we entered, I met Helen. She had suffered a stroke and was confined to her bed. As I walked into her room I noticed her closet door was totally covered with pictures, at least 200. The door was directly in her sight line. After being introduced I asked about the pictures. Were these family and friends? People she knew?

She answered by saying this was her prayer wall. Helen, unable to move, chose to pray. During this time I was deeply vested in self-pity and a self-absorbed mentality. The encounter with Helen cut me to the core of my being. I was brought face to face with my selfishness, ungratefulness, and utter self-centeredness. Leaving her room I had to wipe tears from my eyes. Helen would turn out to be the instrument God used to convict and pierce my soul. Her selfless example would lead me to examine the cave of emotional isolation and self-pity where my heart was making its home.

After our caroling Carl took the children and me to a local restaurant for hot chocolate. There sitting across from each other at the table, he spoke of his personal relationship with Christ. He wasn't preachy or overbearing, but he was openly vulnerable and spoke of Jesus as if He was a real friend. I'm not good with numbers, but I have often wondered what the calculated probability of meeting Carl B Peters would be.

Our first date was New Year's Eve, a dinner date and then a church service. Now I had been to some interesting places on December 31st, but being in a church service was a first! I remember sitting in the service thinking to myself, *Yvonne, you've been in some strange situations before, but this is one of the weirdest yet!* I saw people raising their hands and singing. I heard vocal utterances I did not understand. When the pastor came to the front to speak he wore no clerical collar or suit, but rather a light blue dashiki shirt (this was, after all, the '70s). Nothing about this service was familiar. Everything was strange. I sat nearly frozen in my seat.

As I looked around one woman caught my eye. She was probably in her late forties. Nancy had her arms raised and her eyes closed, but oh my, her countenance was spellbinding. I had never seen such beauty and adoration on a human face. Without words to articulate I sensed this was not a common moment. I saw an "otherness" in worship that captured me. Though I was the perfect storm of pride and fear, this woman's face demonstrated unadulterated calm, peace, and perfect beauty.

"Golden Joinery"

There is an intriguing art form developed by the Japanese as a method for repairing broken ceramics. Knitsugi, translated as "golden joinery," rejoins the pieces of broken pottery by filling the cracks with amalgam mixed with powdered gold, silver, or platinum.[8] The breakage isn't erased but rather enhanced by the golden joining. Knitsugi is built on the aesthetic philosophy of "wabi-sabi," which embraces the flawed and imperfect, revealing instead, the beauty of the broken vessel and featuring the strength in what has been broken.

I was this flawed and imperfect broken vessel, and my Prince was about to begin his "golden joinery" of redemption, filling my cracks with the gold and silver amalgam of his healing. Worship of this amazing God would bond me to the process of His redemption.

WRESTLING WITH SURRENDER

"All who love me will do what I say."
John 14:23

AS A YOUNG believer I was introduced to the third person of the trinity. Surrendering my life to Jesus opened my heart to receive the Holy Spirit, who was now residing "in" me. This was an entirely different concept for me to grasp in the beginning years as a Christ-follower.

The litmus test of our devotion to Jesus is stated by Him when He says, *"Anyone who doesn't love me will not obey me!"* Love and obedience matter if you are going to follow Christ. So an important question at that time for me was, "Did I love Jesus?" And if I answered yes, then how much? Did I love Him enough to obey His truth and direction as revealed through His Holy Spirit who lived in me?

I remember reading the entire Gospel of John in two days following my conversion experience. Three verses were indelibly highlighted for me. John 14:17, *"He is the Holy Spirit, who leads into all truth."* Verse 26, when Jesus is speaking, *"But when the Father sends the Advocate as my representative—that is, the Holy Spirit—he will teach you everything and will remind you of everything I have told you."* John 16:13, *"When the Spirit of truth comes, he will guide you into all truth. He will not speak on his own but will tell you what he has heard. He will tell you about the future."*

If I truly believed these words, would this all–knowing Holy Spirit tell me things to come? Would He take the words Jesus spoke from heaven and speak them again to me? Would the Holy Spirit be the agent, the inner voice who would bring direction to my life? This was extremely heavy teaching for an unchurched girl. But I wanted to believe, and I wanted to obey! Within months of deciding to follow Christ I experienced the first of many "love and obedience" tests. But first a bit of context.

Several months had passed since the first New Year's visit and The Church at Tarpon Springs had become my spiritual community. One Sunday morning an announcement was made in church. There was a need for a kindergarten teacher in the fall. Something in me stirred. There was no audible voice, there were no bells and whistles, no lightning flashes. My senses were simply heightened. As I thought about this and prayed, the inner voice began to speak to my heart. I sensed God was asking me to leave my corporate position and take the job as a pre-school teacher in the small fledgling church school. Loving Jesus and obeying His voice meant leaving the first excellent paying job I'd ever had. It meant letting go of the three-bedroom apartment, the ability to purchase classy clothes and shoes, and hardest of all, disappointing my parents who had sacrificed to provide a good education so I might have an opportunity to succeed financially.

Surrender is a strong opponent, and wrestling with God is a difficult contest you want to lose but fight to the death to win. I wrestled for months desiring to open my hands in love and obedience and follow the Lord's leading, and at the same time, grasping with tightly fisted fingers holding on to what I had. It was an agonizing battle.

There is a parable regarding the capture of monkeys in the wild.[9] Trappers cut an opening in a coconut large enough for the monkey to slip in his hand. They fill the coconut with sweet rice. With fisted hand holding on to the rice the monkey no longer can remove his hand from the coconut. This makes it impossible for him to climb and therefore to escape. The lesson of the parable is simple. To move forward you must surrender, and by necessity, leave behind what holds you captive. I find it interesting that the gesture to receive, an open hand, is the same gesture for surrender, likewise an open hand.

After considerable wrestling with my "sweet rice," I opened my hands to the kindergarten position, and left the corporate world, never to return. I said "no" to the condo and went to live in a small fishing cabin on a lake. I put the purchase of new clothing on hold. Love and obedience won out, but the tests were not over.

Due to my previous corporate job I had managed to save six hundred dollars, a lot of money for me at the time. I proudly opened a personal savings account. Meanwhile there was a large family in the church that appeared in need of financial help. On one Sunday the inner voice, the Holy Spirit, asked me to empty my entire savings, all six hundred dollars, and give it anonymously to this family. What! Another love/obedience test! I would like to tell you I surrendered and obeyed immediately. I did not! But after trying to talk myself out of doing such a crazy thing and processing the request countless times, I obeyed.

There were no immediate results or kudos from men or God for having been obedient. Remember, this was to be an anonymous gift. Unless those fine folks read this book and remember, no one has ever known until now. My reward? I was learning to trust the Holy Spirit who wanted to lead me, and the next steps were important.

There is another story framing this season of my life. It deals with an almost casual remark from the inner voice of the Holy Spirit.

Some months after moving into the one-room fishing cabin, I was outside sitting on the rickety wooden dock in the early evening. My view overlooking Lake Tarpon was becoming one of my favorite spots to simply sit and think. A passenger jet flew overhead and as clearly as if someone next to me was speaking, the inner voice who was becoming familiar to me, spoke these words. *"I am going to send you all over the world." "No way!"* I spoke out loud. While this uncanny discussion may seem strange to you, it was very real to me. Thirty-five years later, having traveled throughout the United States, Europe, the Baltic States, the Caribbean, South America, the Philippines, South Africa, Nigeria, Israel, and the Russian Federation, I must say I think I heard correctly. And oh, what beautiful stories and people I encountered along the journey!

Teaching Bible stories to my five-year-old class, 1979.

My students who taught me unconditional love, 1979.

"I Am Going to Send You All Over the World"

". . . ask and I will give you the nations as your inheritance . . ." Psalm 2:8

TRAVELING TO NATIONS and unknown cultures can be intimidating, or at the very least, uncomfortable. In truth, people are the same whatever nation we find ourselves visiting. As humankind we share the same wants, needs, and desires for ourselves and our families. We all laugh, cry, and experience the range of common emotion given to us by our Creator.

Thankful for all the opportunities to explore and enjoy other cultures, I have collected many stories and gleaned insights along the way. Some stories are funny, some poignant, but all worth the stretch out of my comfort zone. Little did I realize after hearing those words, *"I am going to send you all over the world"* in 1980, I would enjoy such rich experiences making memories lasting a lifetime. I share with you, dear reader, some of my favorites.

East Germany

The year guards left their posts between the eastern and western sectors of Germany, a tour was organized by worship leaders Jim and Anne Mills, along with Kirk and Deby Dearman. All four artists were living as missionaries in Brussels at the time. I received an invitation to participate as a member of the dance company for this ministry assignment. The heart of the mission was to bring the message of hope, encouragement, and the beauty of God's presence to a nation that had suffered greatly. We performed in what once were beautiful cathedrals, now in total disrepair. Because I was an English speaker, a young German woman was assigned to me as a personal translator. We were hosted by the local East German communities that graciously opened their homes to us.

After the concert my translator and I were taken to our host home, a widow who lived alone. Her apartment was very simple, and I was escorted to my bedroom. The "bed" was a human-sized wooden frame with sides and no mattress. It resembled a large kitty-litter box. There was a handmade quilt that served as a coverlet. *Sparse* describes it best. The next morning breakfast was served. The three of us shared one small container of yogurt and one roll, but the small table was covered with a pressed cloth, cut flowers were arranged in a chipped china tea cup, and a small candle was lit. Provisions may have been sparse, but the beauty of hospitality was extravagant. During our conversation I listened to her story. Before the division of Germany in 1961, she and her family had been prosperous. After the great divide, everything was taken from them, everything but the gracious spirit of godly hospitality, which continued to welcome strangers and serve them with beauty and generosity with whatever provisions were available.

Latvia

A few years after gaining its independence from Russia, I was invited to be a member of a church planting team headed for Latvia. Many churches from America were sending missionaries to bring the news of the Gospel to a nation that had heretofore been closed to religious freedom. Latvia is one of three Baltic states located in north-central Europe along the western border of the Russian Federation. The pastors of the team, Bob and Sharon Perry, scheduled a children's workshop for me to teach. Only eight children attended. After giving the children a simple warm-up for their bodies, I taught them some Israeli folk dances. As the workshop ended, I sat them down in a circle and told them the story of Jesus: why He came, how He loves us, what we can do to experience His love personally. The telling was simple and direct. The children showed no emotion; however, one young girl raised her hand to receive the Lord into her life by faith. This young girl, much like the Samaritan woman Jesus met at the well, shared her "Good News" with eighteen members of her family. One-and-a half years later, Bob Perry received from the girl's father a stretched canvas of Vladimir Lenin with this inscription written on the back, *"Bob, this was my god, now I know real God."* Bob graciously gifted me the canvas. I've kept it all these years as a reminder never to underestimate the witness of "one voice."

Performance in East Germany.

Children's workshop Riga, Latvia.

Brazil

And then there is the "red-eye" from Sao Paulo to Rio de Janeiro! The tour of major cities in Brazil had been exhausting. I had in my possession a fake dental apparatus designed as a joke called "Billy Bob Teeth." When in my mouth, these teeth made me look as if I needed extensive dental work. I thought it was a hilarious gag and brought it on tour for use during rehearsals just to make people laugh. Laughter helped defuse exhaustion and any crankiness which might be trying to manifest during an arduous and exhausting tour. I carried these fake teeth in my purse. Our plane had one landing before reaching our destination where we were taking on passengers. I did not want anyone to occupy the seat next to me because I hoped to get some sleep. I put in the teeth before we landed and pretended to be sleeping with my eyes closed and my mouth slightly opened. No one sat next to me! I slept all the way to Rio.

Fun with the "Billy Bob Teeth!"

Guatemala

Affectionately referred to as the "Dirt Dance Tour," Joanne and I, along with Pastor Jeff Ghiotto, traveled to a remote village in the mountains of Guatemala. Our pickup truck carried a portable generator in the cargo bed. The village had no electricity and living conditions were very poor. Our hope was to gather together the people living in the village using the ministry of dance as a tool. Pastor Jeff would bring the Gospel message. Unloading the generator and setting up in the middle of the village drew the attention of the men and women, but it was the music and dancing that drew the children. Our performance space? To be truthful we were side-stepping pig droppings as we danced in the middle of a dirt field. Following Pastor Jeff's message, we walked the village and visited with the people. These beautiful children walked behind Joanne and me, holding up the hem of our costumes, lest they drag on the ground. The honor and respect showered upon us by these barefooted children was a most humbling experience. Grace, honor, and the glory of God were found in the dust and dirt of a Guatemalan village.

Philippines

Beautiful Hannah had been a dancer in the 2001 company at the Feast of Tabernacles in Israel under my direction.

A lovely dancer, I never saw her again until 2015 when I was invited to the Philippines as a keynote speaker for a worship conference. After the Sunday morning service I was invited to have lunch with the pastors and other teachers before we headed to a second service later in the afternoon. During the ministry time at the second service I literally had to dance myself out of a choreography and head for the backstage area where I projectile vomited everything I had eaten a few hours earlier. I wish that had been the end of it, but it was not! I can't remember being so sick from food poisoning. I somehow made it back to the hotel without completely being embarrassed and humiliated in the taxi.

There were several challenges being a sick foreigner in Manila. One, I needed to be hospitalized, because I was severely dehydrated and couldn't keep anything down. Two, Manila is an island. I was scheduled to return to the states in two days. Any visit to a hospital, as a foreigner, would guarantee a quarantine. Not knowing how long they would keep me, I could very well lose the ability to make my flight home. As it turned out, I was to meet Hannah that evening for dinner and a time of catching-up. She ended up coming to me! It turns out Hannah stopped dancing after returning to the Philippines in 2001 and became a doctor. Oh my, I have never been so happy someone stopped dancing to pursue another career! Dr. Hannah set up an IV in my room by driving a nail into the wall and elevating the IV bag above my head. She administered medicine through the IV, stopping the major problems of dehydration. My beautiful Philippine family kept vigil for hours, and sweet Rhoze, my host for the conference, slept next to me all night so I would not be alone. By the next day I was weak, but over the crisis. By God's grace, I kept my scheduled itinerary to teach at the CBN television station the next morning. A miracle!

Writing about some of the more serious stories is much easier than living through them, but I am so much richer for the outcome. Yes, it was uncomfortable. Yes, I was stretched beyond my comfort zone. Yes, I was scared at times. But always, as is God's way, there was care, provision, and most important of all, love. In the Gospel of Matthew 19:20, it says, "*And everyone who has given up houses or brothers or sisters or father or mother or children or property, for my sake, will receive a hundred times as much in return . . .*" These are not just words. They are proven truths in the furnace of testing. These are only a few of the many stories in the span of years in ministry. Let me leave you with a humorous one.

Miami

Traveling in a van during a tour in Florida, worship leaders, Kirk and Deby Dearman, and fellow dancers, José Ramírez-Garza, Valerie Henry, Randal Bane, and I were laughing and enjoying the late-night ride home after a service. Sometime after heading onto the interstate the van caught on fire. Randall stopped near the median and that's when the "crazy" began. We all made it out, and thankfully the van didn't blow up. But it was an "every man for himself" moment! We were stranded on the median, as these were the days before everyone had a cell phone. Waiting to be rescued, we used the time to choreograph and plan the next day of the tour. It was well past midnight and there we were rehearsing dances on the median in the middle of a busy interstate highway! These are memories that make me smile these days.

Tube Tops and Short Shorts: Putting on the Garment of Praise

"Put on your new nature, created to be like God—truly righteous and holy."
Ephesians 4:24

RESURRECTION SUNDAY CELEBRATION plans were approaching at the church, and my friend, Joanne Cecere, asked if I wanted to create a dance as an offering of worship. We spoke to our pastor, Richard Brown, to ask him if this would be a possibility. Richard was very open to the use of dance as our expression of worship for the service. However, he wanted us to be prepared for the backlash we might receive. As a former Baptist preacher, he warned us some people might close their eyes to avoid looking at the dance; some might even complain. I was totally floored! Dance was a part of the expression of joy in my Hispanic culture. Why wouldn't it be an expression of joy in church?

What was there not to like about it? I was confused. He did, however, release us to dance on Resurrection Sunday of 1979. I am forever grateful for the gracious freedom he extended.

More than a girlfriend, Joanne was a spiritual mentor. Though she had only come to faith a year before me, I thought she was the wisest woman I had ever known. She knew everything about God, in my estimation. Joanne had been involved with dance at Hunter College in New York City, while I had little formal training at that time. Hispanic by ethnicity, my cultural filter is very comfortable with dance, so I had the natural propensity and musicality needed. I was confident with being in front of people. In elementary school I participated in plays and variety shows. In junior and senior high school I was a cheerleader. My career in the corporate world involved heading up creative projects for new products. I wasn't afraid to try, and Joanne had more than enough confidence for both of us. We planned our first rehearsal at my apartment.

Carl and Joanne both came to the rehearsal time. I lived in Florida, was not raised in the church or the dance studio, and it was hot and humid! When getting dressed I put on my short shorts, braless tube top, and met them at the door. I don't ever remember Joanne making a remark regarding the inappropriateness of my choices. God only knows what Carl was thinking or had to deal with as he filmed our rehearsal. I still have this aged clip of that first rehearsal, and it continues to make me smile each time I see it!

I share this to encourage you, dear reader. God's criteria for choosing His servants has nothing to do with where He first finds us or how others evaluate us. The "least of these" found in God's choices for his exploits and purposes are too many to enumerate. One of my favorite illustrations is the how and why King David was chosen. Relative to scripture, his brother's credentials certainly outshone those of young David. But God was looking much deeper. He was looking from the inside out. He was looking at the heart of motivation that embodied both love and the willingness to obey.

I had fallen madly in love with this Jesus who delivered me out of depression, hopelessness, and an immoral lifestyle. My God could see my heart and the desire to express that love through movement. Jesus had placed both Carl and Joanne in my life to demonstrate His unconditional, non-judgmental love clothed in human flesh. Grace, amazing grace, was demonstrated by Carl and Joanne. They allowed me to grow without judgment.

Did I stay in inappropriate, immodest clothing for the next thirty plus years of ministry? No! But I am thankful for those first believers God put in my life who could receive me just where I was. Carl and Joanne were more concerned with connection than correction that day.

There is immense worth in demonstrating value. To value is to regard that something or someone is deserving of worth. As created ones who are given breath by the Creator, formed according to His will, and most importantly in His image, we all have great worth.

John C. Maxwell, in his book *Intentional Living: Choosing a Life That Matters* touches on the importance of the intentional practice of adding value to those we encounter daily: friends, family, and stranger alike.[10] As always, Jesus is our role model. He demonstrated value for people—from the woman caught in adultery, to the thief on the cross, from Zacchaeus, a cheating tax collector, to the prodigal who squandered his inheritance. He granted mercy and love to children, murderers, the marginalized, and the rich and entitled. Jesus valued people simply because they had the life of His Father in them.

It is difficult, indeed, to find value in others when we see what is wrong, broken, and out of sorts with what we believe to be righteous and good. But are we going to spend our lives focusing on connectedness or correction? I am so thankful Joanne and Carl chose connectedness.

Joanne was instrumental in directing me to make the reading of God's word a daily priority. Without judgment she brought me to the source of truth. In my immaturity and ignorance some of my first attempts at walking righteously were self-motivated ones. I had several dresses and sling-back high heels left over from my disco days. I got rid of all of them (probably a good call on the apricot knit wrap-around dress). But those heels—I loved them! No matter, I thought they needed to go. I chose to only buy gray and neutral tones for my clothes and wore some awful flat shoes for a time, all in the name of appearing righteous. Unfortunately, I had confused dowdiness with piety.

But my gracious Father several weeks later gifted me with another pair of sling-back high heels through another sister who was clueless as to what I was going through. My standing before a righteous God was not contingent on wearing neutrals and dreadfully ugly shoes. I was righteous because of the sacrifice of the blood of Christ for my sins. While modesty was the plumb line for choosing my personal fashion statement, it was tantamount to put on Christ and His clothing of choice, found in Colossians 3:12, "... *clothe yourselves with tenderhearted mercy, kindness, humility, gentleness, and patience.*"

AUDIENCE OF ONE

"You must not have any other god but me."
Exodus 20:3

BEGINNING WITH OUR first dance on Resurrection
Sunday of 1979, Joanne and I met regularly to train,
rehearse, and craft this dance expression we were using in
worship. We received a few local invitations to share dance
in churches that were moving from traditional liturgical
expressions of worship to more contemporary styles.

In these early beginnings I learned an important ministry lesson that would serve me well for the next thirty
years. It began with an invitation, a fund raiser, for the
Diabetes Foundation. Joanne and I were invited to share
a dance and a brief word of exhortation for those gathered.
The venue for the fundraiser was a sparsely furnished ware-
house called "The Rainbow Garage."

Our ministry, called "SONDANCE," would receive
several calls per month to minister at various events. We
always said "yes!" As young and passionate believers, we

were eager to use our talents to bring God's good news anywhere we were invited. Joanne and I took our ministry assignments and the art of our expression seriously.

We prepared during the week by rehearsing and seeking the Lord as to what encouragement He might want to speak through us to the audience. Arriving early, we marked our dance piece in the space available and checked our music through the sound system. We got dressed and waited for our audience to arrive . . . and we waited, and we waited. An hour past the starting time we realized no one was showing up for the benefit fund raiser. The manager of the venue decided he was going out for coffee and handed us the key. He told us we could wait a bit longer, but to please lock up, leaving the key in a designated area.

We were stunned! We had sought the Lord for both the content of our dance and the exhortation for the people. We realized to leave defeated would be wrong. We made a choice to acknowledge and thank God for what He had given us to minister despite the lack of anyone, other than Himself, being present in the building. We turned on the music and danced before our King! Joanne looked at me and gave me words of encouragement. I looked at her and delivered the exhortation God had put on my heart. We turned off the lights, locked the door, and went out for coffee.

During the next years Joanne and I were invited to minister before hundreds of people in many different nations, and yet the lesson learned in "The Rainbow Garage" significantly sealed my heart with an important spiritual principle. Our approval ratings are never measured by the number of warm bodies present in a gathering. A better metric is the level of trust and obedience to carry out what you believe the Lord has given you to do and to acknowledge "The Audience of One" who is always present and ever watching to perform His word. If we are to have no greater love than the love for God himself, then He is the most important person in the room. He is the King, worthy of all honor, glory, and worship, even when He sits alone.

This lesson has proven valuable when life hits the straights of the mundane, and passion seems to wane. Before "The Audience of One," the mundane becomes sacred, and worship transpires beyond performance. Worship can be expressed in washing dishes, changing diapers, and sweeping floors. I am thankful for that evening. Subsequently, when receiving ministry invitations, I never based my decision to accept on the number of people who might be present. No task too large or small is outside the realm of God's invitation to serve him. "The Audience of One" is enough.

Street ministry in Tarpon Springs, Florida, during the early years.

"Dirt Dance Tour" Guatemala.

Street ministry in Birmingham, England.

Performing in the streets of Honduras.

Reaching out with the Gospel to hundreds of school children
in Honduras.

Gift from God: June 7, 1980

. . . the handsome random stranger, Carl B (no period) Peters who I met in a department store while working for Polaroid corporation, the one who told me about Jesus and invited me to church. That cute blond, blue-eyed guy! He turned out to be the man who asked me to marry him. Until death did we part.

Why Dance Ministry?

"Praise his name with dancing." Psalm 149:3

I'VE OFTEN WONDERED why God chose me to pioneer the ministry of dance and reintroduce this lost expression of worship to the church in my generation. In His sovereignty, He does seem to choose the least likely. If so, I was a good choice! Many times, during these past thirty-nine years I found myself performing with or directing dancers who out-qualified my credentials, experience, and training in the art of dance; and yet there I was. I once asked the Lord, as a sovereign over all things, why hadn't He whispered to my parents to provide dance classes for me, given what He planned to do with my life. The answer He spoke quietly to my heart in response was this: *"I chose to birth you in worship and then teach you to dance."* That, to this day, is my testimony. I am a worshipper of the Most High God who expresses my love to Him through dance.

I did not begin formal training in the discipline of dance until I came to faith in my twenties. This is unheard of in the dance world. Many dancers are wrapping up careers by their mid- to-late thirties. I was just beginning! God provided incredibly gifted teachers and choreographers as tutors, locally in Florida where I was living, as well as international venues in Israel, South Africa, Latvia, and Russia. From 1979 through 1983, I viewed dance as my personal response to God in worship. I had no vision or understanding how this would shape my entire life. Experientially, I knew dance was a valid expression, but what did the Bible have to say about it? I decided to find out.

Genesis 1:2 begins, *". . . and the Spirit of God was hovering over the surface of the waters."* The Hebrew meaning for "hovering" is more correctly translated as moving. The nuances in the original language suggest moving to and fro, fluttering, or shaking and done with the feeling of tender love and care. As I read this narrative of creation, it is easy to imagine Creator God moving "dance-like" over a darkened void ready to bring forth truth and beauty. Though certainly not to the degree of being able to create the universe, as a dancer and choreographer I understand the process of "moving" through space desiring to bring beauty to a concept which communicates truth. It is also interesting to note in Zephaniah 3:17, *". . . he (the LORD) will joy over you with singing."* The primitive root in the Hebrew word for "joy" means to spin and twirl. In both these instances I had no problem connecting with a God who understood dance, and in fact, created it for Himself from the beginning.

The process of choreography involves organizing movement into a meaningful context that can be presented as a cohesive composition. The principles involved in choreography are clearly seen in the Genesis account of creation. For example, examine the adjectives and verbs listed in Genesis 1:1–23, 25:

1—created
2—formless and void, Spirit of God moving over the waters
3—light
4—separated light from darkness
6—expanse in the midst, let it separate
7—contrast between waters below and above
9—let the waters below be gathered into one place
11—earth sprout vegetation
14—separation into seasons, days, years
16—greater light, lesser light
20—waters teem with swarms of creatures, birds fly
25—earth bring forth living creatures, cattle, everything that creeps
28—multiply, fill the earth

Studying these concepts as a choreographer, "separating" waters can be viewed as mirroring—that is, facing each other and doing the same movement. "Separate" or "gathered into one place" suggests contrast—that is, to set side by side to emphasize differences. "Light" and "darkness," as well as, "greater" and "lesser" in the narrative support the contrast principle. "Above" and "below" illustrate the use of levels, so necessary in choreographic works to lend interest. "Teeming" and "flying" support this as well. "Sprouting" and "multiplying" use the idea of expansion, which uses a reoccurring theme the choreographer returns to, along with "contrast," to introduce another perspective to view the work of choreography.

In Exodus 15:20 dance is mentioned for the first time in scripture. The law of first mention is the first time any important word is mentioned in the Bible. This first occurrence establishes the fundamental meaning of the doctrine. In this passage, *"Miriam the prophet, Aaron's sister, took a tambourine and led all the women as they played their tambourines and danced." Mecholah* is the Hebrew word for dance used in the passage. In its first mention, dance is introduced as a response to the deliverance the Israelites experienced when the sea miraculously opened before them. Their escape and rescue from their enemies stirred up a visceral response. Other examples of *mecholah* in the scriptures involved both pure and impure motivation. While Miriam led purely through the Red Sea, there is no mention of who led the dance before the golden calf in debauchery some fifteen or so chapters later. King David is mentioned as dancing uninhibitedly before his God as the "Ark of the Covenant" was restored to Mount Zion—a pure motivation certainly, yet seen as unbecoming and embarrassing for a king by his wife. The fundamental use of dance, however, emanated from a heart of gratitude, thanksgiving, and a desire to glorify the God who brought a great deliverance for His chosen ones.

Old Testament Hebrew and New Testament Greek words are more layered and nuanced than our English translations. For example, the Hebrew words *ealats, giyl, paszaz, chagag, and yadah* are translated simply as "praise," "rejoice," "be joyful," and "worship," rather than the original language, to jump for joy, to leap, to move or march in a circle or procession, to worship with extended hands. In the New Testament, words such as *agalliao,* to jump, to leap, and, *choros,* to dance in the round, are equally descriptive of movement. It was this discovery in study that fueled my desire to reintroduce dance into the culture of the church. The truth of Psalm 149:3, *"Let them praise his name in the dance,"* and the command in Psalm 150:4 to *"Praise him with timbrel and dance,"* was becoming my expressed reality in worship. I was sensing God's nudging to bring those truths to others.

Dance as ministry differs from dance as performed art. I mean no judgment here. I love the art of dance, but not all dance is ministry. Two questions from the Westminster Catechism serve as a litmus test. The first question asks, *"What is the chief end of man?"* The answer is, *"Man's chief end is to glorify God and enjoy him forever."* The second question asks, *"What rule hath God given to direct us how we may glorify God and enjoy him?"* The catechism states, *"The Word of God which is contained in the Scriptures, Old and New Testaments, is the only rule to direct us that we may glorify God and enjoy him."* This catechism was written in 1646 by both English and Scottish theologians with the intention of unifying church doctrine between the Church of England and the Church of Scotland. This creed stands today. Dance as ministry, at its core, is motivated by a strong desire to glorify God, and to glorify Him in the truths presented in His Word.

The very nature of dance requires vulnerability. One must leave self-consciousness behind and fearlessly explore what it means to "communicate" without words. Young children have few problems with this and are natural dancers from the time they can stand on their own. I believe that is why they are such a delight to observe. I think our Father in heaven feels the same way about us. Surrender and vulnerability are the elements of soil necessary for intimacy to take root, and this intimacy grows as we bring more and more of ourselves into God's presence. This requires time spent alone with Him. To dance intentionally as one who ministers to God's people, we bring our physicality, our emotions, our intuitions, our imaginations, our minds, and our life experiences, all of which we are to express in movement. Dancing with all your might through body, soul, and spirit requires surrender. It is dance released from the inside-out. Worship dance emerges because words are inadequate to express our joy, our praise, our desperation, our love, and our longing for the LORD. The answer to the why of dance ministry? Sometimes words are not enough!

From my experience, dancing from the inside-out, or from an impetus authored by the Holy Spirit, has been both spontaneous and choreographed. Trained dancers are innately aware and kinetically connected to their physicality. Core strength, line, nuance, gesture, and musicality are some of the elements absorbed by the dancer through years of training. They are as instinctive as breathing. Moving body parts through space is like inhaling and exhaling. It's what you do when you dance. What "feels" different with dance being led by the Holy Spirit is the connection with the third person of the Trinity. The Holy Spirit, who dwells in all believers who have accepted Christ, is a Master Craftsman and Supreme Choreographer. As the One who moved upon the waters and participated in the artistic expressions of creation, He knows well how to breathe beauty and truth into an atmosphere. Surrendering to the impulse of movement and gesture emanating from the Holy Spirit takes dance to an entirely different level. Returning to our two questions from the Westminster Catechism, no one can glorify the Lord more purely and truthfully than the Holy Spirit. Movement birthed from the Spirit and choreography conceived by the Spirit are quickly discernable. They bring life, not death; truth, not lies; beauty, not crudeness. Dancing from the inside-out requires time preparing in technique classes and equal time developing the spirit of a dancer. There is no way to access the rich deposit of the Holy Spirit's leading in any spiritual endeavor without getting to know Him and learning to recognize the way He communicates with you.

As I consider the many experiences of dancing surrendered to the Spirit's leading, what I treasure most is the pleasure of God in that moment. It is difficult finding words to translate the contentment of bringing pleasure to the God of the entire Universe using the gift He created for you to bring Him glory.

I love the conclusion of Romans 11:36: *"For everything comes from him and exists by his power and is intended for his glory. All glory to him forever! Amen."*

Performing a Holy Spirit–inspired choreography with Father
Alejandro Rodriquez in Israel.

Choreographed dance based on Habakkuk 3:17
with Joanne Cecere in Jerusalem.

Christmas solo to Mariah Carey's, "O Holy Night."

Spanish dance choreographed for an overseas mission trip.

One of many duets with Valerie Henry.

Early photo shoot taken by friend James Ransdell.

Solo work from Feast of Tabernacles celebration in Israel.

With Chloe Osborne Gonzalez during the Exaltation
Conference in Columbus, Ohio.

TO DO OR TO BE

"My old self has been crucified with Christ. It is no longer I who live, but Christ lives in me. So, I live in this earthly body by trusting in the Son of God, who loved and gave himself for me." Galatians 2:20

THE EARLY 1980s was a time of learning and establishing discipline in my life. I made a major change in my career as I transitioned from the corporate world to becoming a kindergarten teacher. I am, by nature, competitive, especially in setting goals for myself. I had a goal to run a hard-and-fast race at becoming the best disciple Jesus could ever desire. Here was the problem: in working this feverish pace, I became a thespian in the circus of performance.

Low self-esteem and insecurity can work through us like yeast works through dough. We can turn inward, becoming insular and fearful of doing anything. In my case, I strived to become a performer; trying to shine and gain the attention

69

and affirmation of those whom we deem influential, powerful, and authoritative is exhausting! As an overachiever and performer, I am ashamed and sorrowful for having made some poor choices and sacrificed important relationships to gain the approval of man. Most grievous are those decisions that affected my family. To "gain ground," I sacrificed time and attention my children needed from me to win the approval of men. I had yet to learn, *"Fearing people is a dangerous trap, but trusting the LORD means safety"* (Prov. 29:25)

A seminar offered by my church, called The Exchanged Life would begin to pry open a new way of thinking and living. Hudson Taylor, a British Protestant Christian missionary to China, first coined the term *exchanged life*. He used this term to expound his message on Galatians 2:20: *"Not I, but Christ or Christ within you."*[11] Bill and Anabel Gilliam, founders of Lifetime Ministries, took this concept and developed a teaching seminar to transform lives. I was one of those students, and Galatians 2:20 would become my life's verse.

The New Living Translation of Galatians 2:20 reads like this: *"My old self has been crucified with Christ. It is no longer I who live, but Christ lives in me. So, I live in this earthly body by trusting in the Son of God, who loved me and gave himself for me."*

What did this mean for me? What does it mean for you? My old self has been crucified; I'm dead! A deathblow has been leveled to my self-striving ways for approval, my self-loathing thoughts and talk, my self-judging and comparisons to others, and my self-consciousness, which makes me the center in all circumstances. As an artist, dancer, and choreographer, these are the ways this self-focused thinking played out in my life. Whatever choreography I created never measured up to my standard. I wanted perfection, "my" ideal of artistic worth and value. Striving was the only way I knew to find perfection.

Let's say I considered the exchanged life message and its ramifications, and I surrendered to the idea, "I'm dead" and no longer the center of my life; then, logically, I would question, "Now what?" Following the logic of this scripture, Christ comes to live in me through the Holy Spirit, and as I trust Him, Jesus lives through me. My self-life begins the transformation process, which I might add, continues until we leave earth.

Please know, even as I write this chapter, I must continue to apply the truth of Galatians 2:20 in every situation. Sometimes I am more successful than others, and unfortunately I lose sight of its truth more often than I'd like to admit. I have had to bring the essence of Galatians 2:20 to mind many times during the writing process and daily to my life's choices. I have not arrived, nor do I completely live in this truth, though I desperately desire to be transformed by it. The truth of Galatians 2:20 brings freedom.

How is this working in me, in real time as I write? Though my self-life is crucified with Christ and I'm dead, if I desire to be obedient to write the book the Lord has placed on my heart, it won't happen magically by just talking about it. My mind and my body must engage in the discipline of writing words. However, herein lies the difference. I write from a place of trust knowing Jesus, through his Holy Spirit, is directing me. My writing begins with this trust factor. If I begin judging myself, comparing myself with myself and others, or engaging in defeating self-talk, then I am paralyzed to move forward. If my goal becomes a striving endeavor to be a best-selling author, to write the most riveting, life-changing book on the market, or to be excellent in order to receive approval and affirmation, then I begin crafting an idol. I am the center of motivation. Because God hates idolatry, I cannot count on Him for any help.

There is an exercise I have adopted from the book, *The Artist's Way* by Julia Cameron and Mark Bryan.[12] I have used it in several of my dance workshops. Here is how it works. I include a series of affirmations and ask students to write them multiple times, much like the old-school technique of writing multiple times why you were being punished for a misbehavior in school. As an example, here is one of my affirmations I review as I write this book: "My dreams and aspirations come from God, and God has the power to accomplish them!" Here is another one I speak verbally before I begin to write: "I can't, but God can!" These affirmations are sometimes followed by the doubting, negative voice of the censor who also tries to set up shop in my head. He says things like, "What about the dreams you had that didn't come to pass?" "Aren't you too old to dream?" "Shouldn't you be settling down?" "Don't dream too big!" But what if Galatians 2:20 grants me the freedom to be obedient to something I sense is from God's heart? What if I trust, by His Spirit, I can write a truthful journey of how surrender forged a heart of worship and transformed a life? What if I let my story speak for itself? What if I let God lead the "whom He desires" to read this book? I am no longer responsible whether it is received or rejected. I am free to "be" me!

And what about you, dear reader? What are you talking yourself out of accomplishing because of fear, rejection, low self-esteem, disapproval, insecurity, or self-judgment? The conclusion of Galatians 2:20 reminds us that the One we have died with now lives in and through us, and He loves us and gave Himself up for us. This amazing proof of love is the only acceptance we need. When we embrace the love of God and the creative parts of our being, we come closer to embodying the design He fashioned us to be.

Now, go be you!

Listening for the Echo

"Make God's glory resound; echo his praises from coast to coast." Isaiah 42:12

THERE IS NO doubt the three-in-one-godhead is mysterious, and many brighter and far more articulate authors and scholars have written about this triune relationship. I remember teaching this three-in-one concept to my four- and five-year-old kindergarteners. In trying to describe the three differences of the one essence, I used the analogy of water having three forms (solid, liquid, and gas), and yet being of one essence. This explanation seemed to satisfy my students, and quite frankly as a new believer, the mystery was beyond my understanding. This simple example satisfied me. I believed it by faith and did not try to dissect it intellectually.

In this present season of life I am grappling to articulate my personal relationship with the Father, Son, and Holy Spirit. I still believe in approaching the mystery of the godhead in childlike faith, but all relationships need review to stay viable. I look to the Father as my covering, my protector, my safety. When I cry, and cry out, "Father God" is what screams from my heart and many times falls from my lips. When I lay my head down at evening, Father is who I ask to hold me. When I am overwhelmed, it is Father to whom I beg for help and mercy.

Jesus is the tangible essence of the Father I see revealed in the scriptures. Without Him, I have no access to the Father. I know Him as the one who died for me, although I find that so hard to imagine. Yet His words and actions say so! In my faith journey during this season I see him most clearly as sovereign King of the Universe, ruling His kingdom from heaven and implementing His strategies on earth. As one called to serve His purposes, I desire to cooperate and walk out my destiny through His plan. Although obedience and faithfulness matter, deeply matter, this sovereign loves me intimately, even when I fail at being obedient and faithful. This brings me incredible security. I am seeking to plumb the depths of this love and to know him as a bridegroom and intimate friend. Desiring to experience this kind of relationship in tangible ways, I am aware this is a lifetime pursuit and will not be fully consummated until I see Him face to face. I look forward to that day.

The sacred Holy Spirit lives in me. I count on Him for all wisdom, all counsel, and direction. He is the one who cares deeply enough to warn me of dangerous thought patterns, unproductive musings, and paths I should not take. Years ago, a wonderful mentor in my life, the late Dr. Sam Sasser, painted a wonderful word picture from his experiences. He was explaining to me how the Holy Spirit works in our lives when we are seeking him for direction. Pulling from his training on a submarine, he went on to tell me that when a torpedo is launched, the screen monitoring its path does not light up significantly if all is well, and the torpedo's trajectory is on target. However, the moment the torpedo ventures even half a degree off course, all the bells and whistles ignite. At the time Dr. Sasser patiently shared this with me I was tormented by my desire to follow the Lord closely and perfectly. The fear of missing the mark Jesus intended, instead of moving me confidently forward, was paralyzing me to move at all. Dr. Sasser's counsel was to relax and trust this amazing gift of the Spirit to warn me if I deviated from the path. If I protected and cherished this relationship, I could walk securely and without fear. A great metaphor, this has anchored my faith.

The amazing Holy Spirit is a gift given to us by the King himself. The Holy Spirit lives in us, leads us, and cheers us on to complete the destiny written for our lives from the beginning of time. He is also expert at magnifying the Son, and I honor and credit Him for any artistic endeavors in my career that have moved the hearts of God's people.

In a recent quiet time, I was pondering the principle of the echo and how it relates to the three-in-one godhead. A true echo is a single reflection of a sound source. If many reflections arrive at the same time, the listener or receiver is unable to distinguish between the reflections. Genesis 1:3 is quite clear God speaks. In truth, He is the source of both light and sound. In the beginning, He spoke the world and creation into existence. He is the source of the echo.

John 5:30 tells us Jesus does nothing by Himself or apart from the Father. *"I judge only as I hear . . ."* Jesus repeats what He hears. Matthew 10:20 states the Holy Spirit can speak the Father's words through us. Because the Holy Spirit lives in us, He can give appropriate answers and guide decisions in the most critical moments. When all the voices and reflections, and there are many, are stilled, and we are quiet, we can hear the echo. God speaks, and through the Holy Spirit makes the words known to us. The Holy Spirit is so familiar to us that many times, we may perceive it as our own voice. Practicing stillness in His presence and consistent deep and healthy doses of reading God's words will verify the authenticity of what we hear. There is no discrepancy between the author of the Word and the echo that comes to your spirit.

Another exercise in *The Artist's Way* by Julia Cameron and Mark Bryan introduces the concept of "morning papers."[13] Morning papers are simply a daily exercise of, upon rising, writing three handwritten pages. The pages are to be written in a stream of consciousness style without thought of paragraphs, punctuation, spelling, grammar, right or wrong, positive or negative comments. Anything and everything that comes to mind is written in the three pages. The pages are never to be read by anyone else. In fact, they might not ever be re-read by the person writing. It is permissible to throw them away when finished.

I have adopted this practice, and one of the immediate benefits is the release of the voices of concern, doubt, and worry that begin to plague us the moment our minds engage in the morning. Many times my morning papers turn into prayer and thanksgiving. The experience is very much like turning yourself upside down and draining your mind of all thoughts. After writing my three pages, I still myself and sit in silence. I tune my heart and mind to listen for the sound from the Father, to be spoken again or echoed with understanding by Holy Spirit, who then speaks to me in exactly the way I can receive.

Our brain's two hemispheres have different functions. The left-brain functionality handles logic, analysis, language, facts, thinking in words, and computations. The right hemisphere thinks creatively, houses the imagination, is intuitive, artistic, rhythmic, and processes nonverbal communication. The right hemisphere is the feeling center of our brain and can visualize and daydream. As humankind we operate in both, but we may have a stronger leaning to one or the other. It is, I believe, the right brain that draws more heavily on developing the ability to hear the echo and the left brain that is grounded securely in scripture. Jesus made it clear in John 10:27; we all have the capacity to hear, if we qualify as sheep! *"My sheep hear my voice, and I know them, and they follow me."* The goal is to have a healthy fusion taking place between the two hemispheres.

Any regular, repetitive action can prime the right hemisphere of the brain. Bathing or showering is said to be an artistic brain activity. This principle is facetiously attributed to Albert Einstein when he rhetorically asked why he seemed to get his best ideas in the shower. Though no Einstein, I have received some of the most powerful images for my choreographic works while soaking in a hot bath of bubbles.

I was asked to prepare an opening choreography for a Passover celebration at a large conference some years ago. As I soaked in the tub, I closed my eyes and began to ponder the story of the first Exodus from Egypt. I tried to imagine the sheer panic and the horrendous cries in Goshen over the loss of so many first-born sons. The house of Israel, by contrast, was totally untouched because of the blood of lambs applied over the threshold of their doors. Not one son was lost! Trying to capture this moment of both solemnity and deliverance, I sensed the Spirit giving me an image. I envisioned a processional with all the first-born sons present at the conference, no matter what age, walking in single file holding fast to a red fabric stretching the entire length of the line. As this image became a choreographic reality on the evening of the event, it turned out some of the first-born fathers bore their own first born sons on their shoulders. An atmosphere of awe was palatable in the room as the conferees observed these fifty-plus men from among them who, because of the blood of the Lamb, were delivered and spared. I discovered the choreography for this simple processional as I listened for the echo.

I have kept written journals since I was sixteen. During the dark years and prior to developing a relationship with Jesus, I would write, sometimes after smoking a joint of marijuana. My journaling, which I thought was so enlightened at the time, was revealed for its true merit by a child. Mine! These journals, even the ugly dark ones, have survived every move I've made. They have been with me in Florida, Georgia, Germany, Washington, D.C., Ohio, and now, once again, in Tampa.

In one of these moves, my young teenager, Zana, was helping me box them up for yet another packing. By this time, I was past all the experimental seeking and was solidly following Jesus. As we packed, she randomly picked up one of the journals and began reading. Of course, it was my writings as the pre-Christ follower, drug-induced, pseudo-enlightened one! She looked at the date it was written and then looked straight at me with her beautiful but incredulously startled eyes and said, "Were you responsible for me when you wrote this?" I looked directly back at her and replied, "Scary, isn't it!" Oh, the wisdom and insight of children. Thankfully the dark period in which the journals were authored did not last more than a few years. God in His mercy protected us all.

I continued journaling through the years, only I listened more and rambled less. These are the journals I treasure for they record the faithful words of the Holy Spirit spoken into my life. These writings have brought incredible comfort during difficult and changing seasons.

Two scriptures I have embraced literally are John 10:27, *"The sheep hear my voice . . ."* and John 16:13, *"[The Holy Spirit] . . . he will speak only what he hears, and he will tell you what is yet to come."* In my journals, I would wait and write what I sensed the inner voice was saying. I would like to share a few excerpts from those early entries and tell you how they ultimately manifested in my life. I desire to share this with you in hopes of encouraging you to believe we can all hear the voice of truth echoed from the Father and Son and spoken by the Holy Spirit in residence within us. Silence and stillness are our friends who prepare the atmosphere for listening. The words received from the listening can feed our souls for years.

This entry was written less than a year after coming to faith and prior to my marriage to Carl on June 7, 1980. I had come through deep repentance and taken responsibility for my past mistakes and failed marriage. Measures of healing were mending my heart, but I was agonizing whether I should remarry. My children had been through so much already. The thought of another relational failure was unbearable. I knew I could never walk through a divorce again. My relationship with Carl was solid, but I was scared. I desperately needed to hear from God. I couldn't say "yes" until I knew that I knew.

November 23, 1979

Carl is for you, my child. You have my assurance in this. I will put you together. My timing is perfect. Continue to trust in me and watch my ways of restoration and healing. They will be of use to you in the ministry I have prepared for you. I meet my people where they are. You continue to love me and praise me always. You will be a light by the example of your life. I love you, my child. I will deliver you from the spirit of inferiority. Remember not the things of old. You are a new creature in Christ Jesus. Allow me to lead, my child. Be careful of nothing, placing all your cares on me.

When reading old journals, I recognize how thirty-eight-plus years of waiting on and listening to the Holy Spirit has changed the tenor and language of His communication with me. With a deepened relationship has come a richer and deeper level of articulation. Yet, I still remember and treasure the simple way He spoke and helped prepare me for what was to come.

Some entries in the early years seemed so nonsensical, particularly the following one.

November 21, 1979

"I had a dream or vision of a small child with red hair."

It must have been a powerful image or I do not think I would have recorded it, and it meant absolutely nothing to me at the time. This entry was tucked away in pencil in the "1979" journal. On February 9, 2010, our only granddaughter, Rylan Pilar Wiseman, was born, and—you guessed it—she is the only redhead in our Hispanic family. Coincidence? Perhaps. I choose to believe the God of the entire universe desires to be intimately aquatinted with each of us, and it pleased Him to share His secret with me. He is all knowing, and if we listen, desiring to hear and willing to obey, we just might get a glimpse of what lies beyond.

Gift of laughter from my dance partner: Latvia, 1990s

We were on tour together in Latvia getting ready to dance in an old dilapidated church. As part of the former Soviet Union, Latvia had recently declared its independence on May 4, 1990, and the bathroom in this church hadn't been cleaned since the Romanovs ruled! You went in first. As you came out, I asked how bad it was. Without expression you simply replied, "Fourth position plié, contraction." Ah! Dance humor.

Dreams, Paintings, and Artists

"And God came to Laban in dreams by night ..." Genesis 31:24

I AM NOT prone to volumes of dreams, but there have been a few unforgettable ones. A dream in the 1990s was so powerfully vivid, I recorded it in my journal upon waking. It was quite disturbing, but when nothing seemed to come from it, I packed it away, and the journal made at least six more moves before I read it again.

In this dream I was frantically trying to save all my loved ones from an impending storm rising over the horizon. An enormous mountain range before me was being enveloped by dark, stormy, ominous clouds that were moving closer and closer. A large high-rise with one entire side of its facade made of glass, made it possible to be sheltered while watching the storm coming toward us. I had successfully, though under great distress, gathered all my loved ones, including Carl, into the glass-sided high-rise. And then I looked out. Carl had somehow escaped from the building and, with a staff in hand, was headed straight up the mountain into the storm.

I was paralyzed with fear and enraged with anger at the same time. How could he do this to me? And what was he doing? We hadn't talked about this or agreed to this. I tried so hard, gave it my all to keep him safe, and now he was headed into the storm. As the clouds loomed thicker and darker, they began to encompass Carl. Then out of nowhere a strange light illuminated a break in the clouds. As I looked I could see Carl dancing wildly on the summit. For those of you who saw Richard Gere in his role of King David bringing back the Ark of the Covenant to Israel in the 1985 movie, this image of Carl dancing was quite similar. And then I awakened.

The images were so powerfully imprinted in my imagination that they remain vivid and potent even as I write today. I didn't understand the dream. Carl was quite independent, and I'm sure I wrote this off as a reinforcement of my personal judgment of his quiet stubbornness. It wasn't until his death in 2012, as I reread old journals, I came upon the entry again.

All at once what I could not understand suddenly seemed so clear. Oh, how I wanted my husband, the love of my life, to live and not die! I desired more years together. In faith and prayer, with cries and tears of mercy, submitting to homeopathic care and experimental treatments, through all possible means, I tried to prolong his life. But in the end, God called him home, and I could only watch him face this incredible challenge bravely and head-on. Revisiting the journal and remembering the joy and freedom in the image of him dancing, brought a measure of comfort in the grieving.

Happenstance? I don't think so. Beyond words are images, pictures, art, and dreams—all the substance of nonverbal communication. These indelible impressions are stored in the inner spirit of man when words are not enough. God himself demonstrated this principle of pictorial communication with his servants and in His creation. The display of the rainbow stretched across the sky is one such example.

Imagine yourself in Noah's sandals. Prior to the flood, no one had ever seen rain. The earth, according to Genesis 2:5–6, was watered by *"streams [which] came up from the earth."* Water had only come from the bottom up. What a shock to suddenly experience water descending from the top down! Once Noah weathered the flood, what assurance did he have this very same scenario wouldn't repeat itself every time something bad went down? Verses later,

God assures Noah the earth will never again be destroyed by flood waters, but He gives him an image to remember. In God's creative act to commemorate and establish a new beginning, a new covenant, a new promise, He paints a rainbow on the canvas of space and sky.

God chooses to speak through the art He creates and the artisans He has created. There is power in imagery and its ability to awaken emotion and clarify thought. It was the power of imagery that resuscitated my dying soul in 2001.

This challenging season in my life paralyzed me for a time. My marriage, ministry, finances, and relationships were shipwrecked. A parachurch ministry assignment in Washington, D.C. ended abruptly and left me devastated. Carl and I headed back to Tampa with no source of income, huge debt, and heavy hearts.

I hadn't been to a doctor for a checkup in some time, so I made an appointment. As I lay on the examining table I glanced up. The clever doctor had placed a painting on the ceiling. As I stared into the print, I began to weep. I later found out this was John William Waterhouse's "Miranda the Tempest" painted in 1916. I was transfixed. All the angst, anger, and sorrow I had tried to bury and render numb was exposed and awakened. Through the painting, I found a thread of hope. It was the first glimmer in a year.

The painting captures a beautiful young woman standing on the rocky shore of an ocean. Though peacefully serene, she appears to be staring at the remains of a capsized ship ready to sink. Debris from the wreckage can be seen floating near her feet. Three points of a red fabric are seen peeking through her long midnight-blue dress. These three visible points of red appear near her ear, her hand, and her feet. As I gazed at the painting I remembered a passage from scripture. *"The priests will then take some of the blood of the guilt offering and apply it to the lobe of the right ear, the thumb of the right hand, and the big toe of the person being purified"* (Leviticus 14:14).

I have no idea what muse John Waterhouse was contemplating as he painted Miranda. What I know is his art awakened me from numbness. I could feel again, and feeling led me to thinking, and thinking led me to truth. If you look closely at the painting, it appears Miranda is with child. Life would emerge from wreckage.

In the few minutes before my examination, a glimmer of hope returned. The trial was over. What was destroyed was not ultimate tragedy. The blood offering for purity and consecration to the priests during the time of Moses was a type and shadow of the blood offering purchased by Christ and available to me. I needed purified ears, hands, and feet to move forward. Unforgiveness had taken a stronghold over my heart. Like Miranda, there was hope of new life for the coming season. Everything was not lost.

After telling Carl of my experience in the doctor's office, he later made an appointment with the gynecologist. Imagine her surprise! He, of course, only wanted to see the examination room. He took note of the print and gave it to me for Christmas. It hangs in the entry way of my home. Oh, that we understood and were mindful of the many intimate ways God communicates with us.

One more story before I bring this chapter to a close. In 2010, Carl and I resigned from our long-standing ministry with the International Christian Embassy Jerusalem. Along with other dance company members, Carl and I performed a final dance/drama piece on the convention stage. During rehearsals, David Stott, a longtime friend and photographer, captured a photo of me in a very dramatic back fall. It was later posted on Facebook where my beautiful friend, Ismarily Velazquez from Puerto Rico, discovered it. I have asked her to tell the story of how she married her art and intercessory prayer on our behalf.

> *For every season in life, God prepares our*
> *hearts surrounding us with people who*
> *inspire and challenge us to be better. This is*
> *the case of Yvonne and Carl. The way God*

orchestrated how we met was unique and interesting. I remember sometime in 1995, I received a phone call from my boyfriend (now husband) telling me of this amazing dancer who was giving workshops at a worship conference in Florida and that I needed to meet her. He told me her name was Yvonne Peters and that it would be a good idea to invite her to Puerto Rico. Three days later, I found out Yvonne was one of the guest speakers at the workshop I was attending. The first time I saw her I knew instantly she was the perfect person for our school. I was in love with her heart and sweet spirit. The wisdom and revelation in her from God (Exodus 31:3) was exactly what we were praying for during that time. The connection was immediate, and we started planning for her and her husband to come to Puerto Rico.

Two years later, Yvonne and Carl came to Puerto Rico. Their work in our church with the youth and adults was just excellent. She was a beautiful dancer who put movements to the words, and he was an actor, always

*creating and acting a character in his per-
formances. Artists from different churches
around the island came to these workshops
offered by them and other talented instruc-
tors. Today I still hear testimonies of what
God did to their hearts during that time.*

*Yvonne and Carl were both a great example
of what marriage must be, and what it's
about. If you find Yvonne, you will find Carl.
They were inseparable. Even though we never
enjoyed a close friendship because of the distance, we always kept a special connection .
. . the kind of connection that only God can
do. Sadly, several years later, we found out
that Carl was fighting a terminal cancer. I
remember that day. The news was heart-
breaking, and it hurt my soul that I could
not be there to comfort her because the distance did not allow me to do so. I did one
thing I knew I could do—pray.*

*At that time, I was doing a live painting each
week on a set at IHOP (International House
of Prayer) so I turned my painting/prayer*

time on behalf our friends. I always enjoyed painting dancers, so this time I used a photograph of Yvonne dancing. For two hours, I prayed and painted; while I was asking Jesus for His love, grace, and favor. While I was painting, the worship leader at the moment, Misty Edwards, was singing these words: "Don't let my love grow cold, don't let my passion die." I was crying while the oil paint simultaneously was dripping onto the canvas. I remember praying specifically for Yvonne's heart, that this trial would not allow bitterness and coldness to enter in her heart or get offended. I knew I needed to keep praying for Carl, but in that moment my prayers turned toward Yvonne's heart. It was a prayer for her to receive new strength.

Sadly a few months later, we found out that our friend Carl passed away. His sweet spirit, creativity, and ability to bring laughter and joy to those around him will be missed. We cried, but with hope that we will someday see him again. Love always leaves a memory no one can steal and there are so many memories

that I know Carl has left in so many hearts.
He will never be forgotten.

How utterly profound! The grief of losing Carl was so deep I wasn't sure I could ever recover. The prayer from the heart and brush of this artist, *"Don't let my love grow cold, don't let my passion die"* was heard and answered. The pain of grief is real, but likewise are the promises of hope, comfort, and healing. My love for God has not waxed cold, and the flames of my passion have been fanned. Oh, the beauty of God's artists who serve Him with the gifts He so graciously bestows. This framed print hangs in my home, a constant reminder of the power of artistry, image, and prayer.

Hanging Out in Corner Four

"He that dwells in the secret place of the Most High . . ." Psalm 91:2

DANCE HAD BEEN a creative outlet for me as a child playing alone in my aunt's living room, as part of my Hispanic culture, as a means of escape from reality, as a tool of sexual allure, and as an expression of worship. It has provided both joy and pain, exhilaration and defeat.

Recently I heard an incredibly insightful lecture by Dr. Henry Cloud, a clinical psychologist. His talk centered on relational connectedness. In an interesting illustration he drew a box with a number one beginning in the upper left-hand corner, and continuing clockwise reaching corner four. Corner one represented relational isolation. I personally call this corner the "cave of self-pity." Dwelling in this isolated cave seems to offer solace and protection, but it produces no fruit in life and no lasting comfort or relational connectedness.

Leaving corner number one, we may venture to corner two. It is in this corner we berate ourselves and develop self-loathing, guilt-producing self-talk. *"I am a loser." "I'm bad." "Who would ever love me?" "This is yet another failure."* Unable to bear corner two for any length of time, we back track to corner one for another dose of isolation, or perhaps move to corner three. Corner three is designed to relieve the pain produced by corners one and two. This is the "faux" good corner. Whatever brings escape, distraction, or numbness is practiced here: drugs, alcohol, sex, gluttony, overworking, not working, excessive gambling, excessive gaming, movies, and TV, just to mention a few.

Sadly, I spent a great bit of my childhood and young adult years bouncing between these three corners. I lived in corners one and two most of my failed marriage. Venturing into corner three to escape self-reflection was my downfall, but thankfully I landed on my knees.

I didn't discover corner four until I met Jesus, and even then, the inroads to my comfortable corners were so engrained, it took time and time again refusing to go there. When enough pressure comes into my life, the temptation to visit these deadly corners remains, though I now have tools in place to fight going there.

Access to corner four necessitates admitting and articulating you have a need and in humility asking for help. This is the corner of genuine connectedness. This is the corner of dependence on God. This is the corner of interdependent relationships. This is home plate where we are safe.

Would I could boast upon discovering corner four I never again left its safety. That would be a lie. Being involved in ministry and working with others in ministry is a "people business" culture. Our brokenness breaks through all the time. In our pain and disappointment, we can easily move into isolation, self-loathing, and self-gratifying escapes. Being in ministry does not provide a privileged, high-towered dwelling place for me. But beyond our fears is connectedness to the One who loves us unconditionally, who provides relational connectedness to others, and these others grow us, challenge us, support us, bring life to us. They, along with God, hang out in corner four.

BEING CONTENT WITH YOUR PORTION

"The land you have given me is a pleasant land. What a wonderful inheritance!"
Psalm 16:6

IT IS INTERESTING to observe the free role play of children. Reflecting on the ways that my daughter Zana played is a prophetic decree on her life's accomplishments. As a child, she would line up her many stuffed toys in a very orderly arrangement around her room. They would become her audience, or students, or friends, whatever she needed them to be. She also loved—absolutely loved—nurturing her dolls. One such doll had a velvety covering resembling real skin. She loved the fuzz off that doll! Today Zana is one of the most incredible mothers I know. She is also a principal in the education system of Florida as an extremely talented and qualified leader and administrator. Her "play" revealed the DNA of her destiny and call.

Rob, my son, played very well alone, if he had action toys. Yellow Tonka trucks were his favorite. He also spent inordinate amounts of time working with my father, who was a cattle rancher. Rob was riding solo on a horse by age four and learned to drive a truck before he was ten! Rob's play not only included moving trucks around in his room but experiencing the action of driving tractors in real-time, and the responsibilities entailed working on the ranch with my father. Today Rob continues to pursue adventure and is one of the most responsible adults I know. An avid scuba diver and spearfishing aficionado, he is a good husband and father. But he still needs alone time.

For those reading this book who are parents, pay attention and learn how to undergird and encourage those small ones in your care. God reveals who He has created us to be and can disclose the blueprints of our DNA in playtime.

I was always organizing plays or shows as a child in my neighborhood. I would hang a shower curtain on the clothesline outside in the yard and invite the neighborhood kids to come over. Of course, I would direct and make up scenarios on the spot. In the school yard during recess, for any of the children who had not selected a game to play or who seemed too shy to make known their desires, I had a plan. I gathered them up and showed them what we could do! Arranging them in a straight line under the pine trees, hopefully they were comfortable on the soft pine needle beds beneath them, they became my audience. It was here I would teach them. What? I have no idea, but I talked and taught whatever came to mind. A miracle, they never moved until recess was over. It is not surprising then to see how this free play has shaped the DNA of my destiny and call.

Many times during my later elementary school years I was chosen to be a narrator in school plays or in acting roles for various skits. One of my dreams was to direct and star in the role of Cinderella, an unlikely heroine whose beauty was restored from the ashes and drudgery of being unloved. The stories and fairy tales we love as children are also very telling of how we see ourselves in the deepest parts of our being.

I had the perfect dress for the role of Cinderella and desired the part desperately. Here was the problem: I wasn't the director. My friend Jeanette beat me to the project, and she had another Cinderella in mind, my other friend, Donna! I was crushed. I felt the part was mine, made for me. I can't remember what part Jeanette cast me in, because I never filled that role. Unfortunately for Donna, and fortunately for me, Donna came down with the measles. Though not first choice, I did get to play the part of Cinderella in the third-grade play.

There are times when pivotal events are forever locked in our memory banks. I can't remember where I put my phone down most of the time, yet I can still remember the smoky blue taffeta and nylon net dress left over from some wedding. It was just my size! This is the dress I donned to the Cinderella ball. Sadly, I also remember never empathizing or sympathizing with Donna. It was all about me getting what I wanted, no matter how it was achieved.

I scored a win to my own selfish desires at the cost of someone's misfortune that day. However, there have been many times since third grade I have failed to gain what I tried to attain. In some cases, a measure of maturity was reached and greater character was formed. In other cases, there was internalized hurt, resentment, depression, and self-pity—lots of self-pity.

There is a character revealing story in 1 Samuel, chapter 2, which has always attracted my attention.

> *Now the sons of Eli were scoundrels who had no respect for the Lord or for their duties as priests. Whenever anyone offered a sacrifice, Eli's sons would send over a servant with a three-pronged fork. While the meat of the sacrificed animal was still boiling, the servant would stick the fork into the pot and demand*

that whatever it brought up be given to Eli's sons. All the Israelites who came to worship at Shiloh were treated this way. Sometimes the servant would come even before the animal's fat had been burned on the altar. He would demand raw meat before it had been boiled so that it could be used for roasting.

The man offering the sacrifice might reply, "Take as much as you want, but the fat must be burned first." Then the servant would demand, "No, give it to me now, or I'll take it by force." So, the sin of these young men was very serious in the lord's sight, for they treated the lord's offerings with contempt.

Hophni and Phinehas were the wicked sons of Eli the priest. These spoiled boys were granted their every whim and were undisciplined in curtailing their selfish desires, even regarding the Lord's holy offerings. They simply disregarded the laws of offering prescribing the fat be burned as a sweet aroma to the Lord before consuming the sacrifice. The wicked sons of Eli took what they wanted regardless of protocol, with no fear of the Lord.

Being discontent with God's "no's," if handled in ungodly ways, circumvents and delays the maturity needed to walk in God's plan for our lives. Should we be promoted because of someone's misfortune, it's best not to let pride get a stronghold. For the mysterious workings of God, give thanks and remain humble. If we have been spared or favored, it is grace-filled favor for which we offer thanks.

There is resident in human nature a propensity for the more and the immediate. When both fail, discontent is an uninvited guest who never knows when it's time to move on. Humility and gratitude are the only bouncers who can get rid of them. I wish I could find Donna today. I'd like to tell her I am sorry she could not play Cinderella. I'd like to ask her forgiveness for never giving her a thought as I played the role I thought I deserved.

Gift from Carl:1990s

What were you thinking? I'd like to ask that question of you. Surely giving me a 410, over-and-under rifle for Christmas was a bad idea. I didn't even like guns, much less want to shoot one! You loved to give gifts "you" wanted others to have. It makes me smile now. But not then. Worst Christmas gift ever!

P.S. Thank you for giving me your gifts of kindness, protection, provision, and laughter.

If the Root Is Holy, So Are the Branches

"But some of these branches from Abraham's tree—some of the people of Israel—have been broken off. And you Gentiles, who were branches from a wild olive tree, have been grafted in." Romans 11:17

AS I MENTIONED earlier, I was not aware of my Jewish roots in 1983 when I made my first trip to Israel. On the final day of the tour our guide took us to the Western Wall prior to departing for the airport. As I stood in the women's section with my face to the ancient stone wall, I began to weep. Spiritually and emotionally there was such a connection with the land and the people. I was certainly grateful for the opportunity to be there, but I couldn't imagine never being able to return. I had no idea I would only have to wait a year!

One eye-opening revelation of being in the land of the Bible was recognizing the context where the scriptures were received. As an immature believer, my tendency was to pick and choose passages from the Word of God and apply them to my need or desire. Touching, tasting, smelling, and seeing the land where God birthed His nation collided with my white, Western cultural church filter. Suddenly I was confronted with the possibility God's promises weren't solely applied to me. The prosperity "Name It, Claim It" gospel was a popular teaching at the time. After the extensive two-week tour and Jewish history lesson from the call of Abraham to the regathering of the nation in 1948, I wasn't sure I had it right. The promises I so readily embraced were given to the Jews first, and if I believed they were "yes and amen" for me, then they were still "yes and amen" for them. Israel had not been cast aside permanently, as some teachings professed. If that were true, then how secure were the promises I held to?

Romans 11 is Paul's perfected discourse on the attitude, as Gentiles, we are to maintain regarding Israel. According to Ephesians 2:14–16, *"Christ himself has brought peace to us. He united Jews and Gentiles into one people when, in his own body on the cross, he broke down the wall of hostility that separated us. He did this by ending the system of law with its commandments and regulations. He made peace between*

Jews and Gentiles by creating in himself one new people from the two groups. Together as one body, Christ reconciled both groups to God by means of his death on the cross, and our hostility toward each other was put to death." In Romans 11, however, we are given a glimpse into the unfathomable wisdom of God's plan. The verses in chapter 11 were like small pricks begging for more thought and study.

Prick #1 from Romans 11:13–16:

> *I am saying all this especially for you Gentiles. God has appointed me as the apostle to the Gentiles. I stress this, for I want somehow to make the people of Israel jealous of what you Gentiles have, so I might save some of them. For since their rejection meant that God offered salvation to the rest of the world, their acceptance will be even more wonderful. It will be life for those who were dead! And since Abraham and the other patriarchs were holy, their descendants will also be holy. Just as the entire batch of dough is holy because the portion given as an offering is holy. For if the roots of the tree are holy, the branches will be, too.*

Because of God's sovereign choice, the Jews are his elect, his chosen ones. In addition, because God is holy, and using the metaphor of a root system as a picture of God's holiness, then any branches growing from the root are holy. Paul continues with a warning to the Gentiles regarding pride that might surface because of this election.

The metaphor of root and branches paints a vivid picture. Those to whom Paul was speaking knew much about horticulture. Yes, it was possible, though difficult, to graft wild olive branches into cultivated trees, and this was happening spiritually. Salvation was no longer solely for the Jews. The sacrificial death of Jesus made it possible for all to enter the salvation experience—Jew and Gentile alike.

However, and here is Paul's point and prick #2, as wild olive branches the Gentiles needed to guard their hearts from pride. Branches, wild or cultivated, never support the root! Paul warns, *"But you must not brag about being grafted in to replace the branches that were broken off. You are just a branch, not the root. "Well," you may say, "those branches were broken off to make room for me." Yes, but remember, those branches were broken off because they didn't believe in Christ, and you are there because you do believe. So, don't think highly of yourself, but fear what could happen. For if God did not spare the original branches, he won't spare you either."*

Paul concludes with an arresting statement in verse 29, prick #3: *"As far as the gospel is concerned they (the Jews) are enemies on your account; but as far as election is concerned they are loved on account of the patriarchs. For God's gifts and his call are irrevocable."*

Scriptures from Old Testament prophets lend support to Paul's claims such as Jeremiah 10:16, *"But the God of Israel is no idol! He is the Creator of everything that exists, including Israel, his own special possession."* And there is a more extensive passage from Jeremiah 31:35–37: *"It is the Lord who provides the sun to light the day and the moon and stars to light the night, and who stirs the sea into roaring waves. His name is the Lord of Heaven's Armies, and this is what he says: I am as likely to reject my people Israel as I am to abolish the laws of nature! This is what the Lord says: Just as the heavens cannot be measured and the foundations of the earth cannot be explored, so I will not consider casting them away for the evil they have done. I, the Lord, have spoken!"*

What do Romans and Jeremiah have to do with being a Christ-follower, a worshipper of God?

The answer lies in desiring to love what God loves, to pay attention to what gets His attention. He loves the nation He called out to be his own possession.

To more fully understand the Messiah I loved, the Messiah who saved me from myself, I considered His earthly ethnicity. Jesus was a Jew. While Jesus offered the gift of salvation to the world, He repeatedly said He had come to His own people. In Matthew 15:24 He declares the mission, *"I was sent only to help God's lost sheep, the people of Israel."* Jerusalem was the only city He wept over.

The existence of Israel as a nation is a plumb line attesting to God's faithfulness. There are no more Hittites, Amorites, or Jebusites on the planet. However the one nation and people called out by God still exists! Israel remains a nation, and her capital city is Jerusalem, the city to which Jesus will return. The security regarding God's promises to His ancient people throughout history undergirds His promises to me. Because He has not failed Israel, He will not fail me. And the constant care and regard for truth He has spoken fuels my heart of worship for a God who does not change. He has the power to fulfill His word to His ancient people, to me, and to you!

Unforgettable Rehearsal

*"The Lord God placed the man in the
Garden of Eden to tend and watch over it."*
Genesis 2:15

REHEARSALS ARE A prerequisite for most any event, be it dance concerts, weddings, or graduations. Any public invitation to view a performance calls for a rehearsal. One rehearsal in Israel is unforgettable.

It was Jerusalem in the late 1980s and, as dancers, we were rehearsing a processional scheduled for one of the evenings of the Feast of Tabernacles celebration. And rehearse this processional we did, every day for almost two weeks.

On the evening we were to perform there was a sudden programming change. For unknown reasons this well-rehearsed processional was being eliminated from the program. Why this was changed I never found out. What I learned from it I never forgot.

Backstage I engaged in a conversation with the Lord about this situation. I said something like this, "God, you know all things. You even make donkey's talk. If you knew this piece was going to get cut, couldn't you have told us about it? If we'd had knowledge, we could have put our time into rehearsing the other dance choreographies." In my immaturity, I thought this was a reasonable conversational exchange with God. What I heard in my inner most being as God's response, felt as if the air was being sucked out of my lungs. And like Job, felt *"My ears had heard of you, but now my eyes have seen you."* Though there was no physical "seeing," an aspect of the glory and holiness of God was revealed. This is what I heard from the quiet inner voice of the Holy Spirit. "Who are you to decide when I take my offerings. If I choose to take my offering in rehearsals, that must be enough for you." I was stunned!

Our New Testament offerings of worship are spiritual sacrifices. There are seven spiritual sacrifices mentioned in the Bible, but two of them pertain to giving praise and thanksgiving to God simply for who He is. Romans 12:1 says, we are to offer our entire lives: body, soul, and spirit. *"And so, dear brothers and sisters, I plead with you to give your bodies to God because of all he has done for you. Let them be a living and holy sacrifice, the kind he will find acceptable. This is truly the way to worship him."* Worship dancers take this seriously. Our prayer is to offer, in excellence, a demonstration through our movements. And while this is the intent of our hearts, one of the weaknesses in the soul of a performer is to evaluate worship on how, when, and who sees the demonstration. These, I might add, are weak and improper metrics to measure an offering to God. God's words to me in that moment cut deeply into the motivation of my heart. He was saying, if I believed my dance was a spiritual offering, then whether He received it in rehearsals or the actual worship event, it should not affect me, at all! In fact, it was His offering, His gift to receive, and that gave Him the right to accept it whenever He desired. My concept of being in rehearsals and running rehearsals was forever altered. Practicing with the awareness of His presence was the main event. Recognizing the omnipresence of God in all my endeavors recalibrated my attitude.

Genesis 2:15 reads, *"The Lord God placed the man in the Garden of Eden to tend and watch over it."* In Hebrew, the word for *work* and *worship* are interchangeable. The Hebrew word *abad* means both "to work" and "to do," as well as, "to serve" and "to worship." I learned these lessons being a worshipper expressing my love for God through dance. But, beyond the dance was the truth that even the most menial tasks can become worship when given back to God in praise and thanksgiving as a spiritual sacrifice. God receives these expressions of love whether others are watching or He is the only one in the room.

"Oh, how great are God's riches and wisdom and knowledge! How impossible it is for us to understand his decisions and his ways! For who can know the LORD'S thoughts? Who knows enough to give him advice? And who has given him so much that he needs to pay it back? For everything comes from him and exists by his power and is intended for his glory. All glory to him forever! Amen. (Romans 11:33–36)

Gift from Prime Minister Ariel Sharon:
Fall of 2001

You, Prime Minister, had given your wel-
come speech to the pilgrims at the Feast
of Tabernacles. I watched the protocol as
your guards escorted you from the building.
The agents in front of you walked straight
ahead, as the agents to the sides of you were
looking incessantly in all directions. It was
the agent behind you who caught my atten-
tion. He was the only one walking backward,
his back facing your back. I understood for
the first time what Isaiah meant when he
penned, "[T]he God of Israel will be your
rear guard." I saw, I understood. The Son
of God positioned Himself to take the "hit"
intended for me.

Isaiah And Israel's IDF

"And as the Lord strikes them with his rod
of punishment, his people will celebrate with
tambourines and harps." Isaiah 30:31

TWENTY-SIX YEARS OF ministry in Israel has provided me with not only great memories and lasting friendships, but many faith-building moments. One in particular occurred in the early 1990s.

There was more tension than usual in the Middle East due to the Gulf War. Rehearsals for the Feast of Tabernacles celebration were proceeding well. By all accounts the morning began typically with early breakfast and rehearsals for the evening's presentation. This night's program was slightly different from the other nights, for thousands of Israelis were invited as our guests. Several popular musical artists had been invited, among them Grammy Award–winning singer Ricky Skaggs.

Our rehearsal hall was very near the Old City of Jerusalem, and though during the morning we kept hearing sirens, we paid very little attention. An hour later we received the news. A serious disturbance with loss of life had occurred in the Old City.

It seemed several Palestinian insurgents had stormed the Old City setting the Israeli police station on fire. Proceeding into the city, these men perched themselves atop the sixty-two-foot ledge overlooking the Western Wall, Israel's holiest prayer site. HaKotel, as it is called in Hebrew, is the last vestige of a retaining wall built by Herod the Great around 19 BCE. It is here where Jewish men donned in prayer shawls, gather for prayer. And it was here, on this fall morning, the Palestinians began to hoist fifty- to-sixty-pound rocks on the heads of the unsuspecting Jewish worshippers. In the heat of the moment, as Israeli police gained control of the situation, several of the insurgents were fatally wounded. Fortunately, and miraculously, none of the Jewish men were maimed or lost their lives.

It was amidst this background a decision from the directors of the event had to be made. Should we proceed as planned or cancel? The evening's celebration was to occur outdoors in the Sultan's Pool venue, and as I mentioned, we were expecting thousands of guests from the community. Let me take a moment to explain the site of this venue.

Sultan's Pool is located right outside the Old City Walls. It is situated in the Valley of Hinnom, which is a deep, narrow ravine located in Jerusalem running south on the west side of the Old City, then eastward along the south side of Mount Zion until it meets the Kidron Valley. If you have never been to Jerusalem, this will mean little to you, so let me translate. Anyone going down into this area, which is where the seating and stage areas were located, is a "sitting duck" when it comes to security.

Certainly the leadership had some very serious decisions to make. Meanwhile, I too had a decision to consider. If we received a "yes," indicating we were going forward with the evening, would I have the courage to proceed knowing full well the gravity of the security situation?

One of the strongest convictions of my faith is the belief in the absolute sovereignty of God. Innately I knew none of this had taken the God of the entire universe by surprise. However, that did not dispel my fears and anxious thoughts. The call came. We were proceeding with the event. Amid uncertainty and adversity, we would worship the God of Israel.

I remember the apprehension in my heart as I walked to Sultan's Pool late in the afternoon. Rehearsals were to take place at 5:00 PM. As I descended the valley and made my way to the stage, I looked up to see the entire perimeter rimmed with Israeli Defense Forces. Gigantic search lights were being brought in for added security. The little chubby girl from 3019 East Louisiana Avenue could never have imagined herself being in this situation!

As the dancers walked into the valley and up to the stage there was silence. No one spoke to each other. There was none of the usual laughter and goofing around. The mood was somber. The entire worship team—dancers, singers, musicians and speakers—had been extended the choice to participate or stay back. All the dancers chose to come. Though there was some level of fear, the dance company remained committed. In faith, we had been called to Jerusalem to love and worship our God with all our hearts, with all our souls, with all our minds, and with all our bodies. We were prepared to complete the assignment.

Rehearsals went well. Once we focused our attention on the evening before us, we began to relax, trust the excellent security of the IDF, and wait for the evening to begin. With the first refrain of the evening's opening praise song, a passage from Isaiah 30 I had read earlier was quickened to my mind.

> "At the Lord's command, the Assyrians will be shattered. He will strike them down with his royal scepter.
>
> And as the lord strikes them with his rod of punishment, his people will celebrate with tambourines and harps. Lifting his mighty arm, he will fight the Assyrians. Topheth—the place of burning—has long been ready for the Assyrian king; the pyre is piled high with wood."

I was reminded once again like the armies of old, God was using His worshipping singers, dancers, and musicians to strike down the enemy. Though Assyria was mentioned as a literal enemy of Israel in the Isaiah scripture, metaphorically, God was again using the sounds of worship to come against the present fear that had permeated the day's tragedy.

One morning, a few months later, as I was studying Isaiah 30:31, I became aware that the Valley of Topheth mentioned in the scripture was synonymous with the Valley of Hinnom where our worship event was held that fateful night. They were, indeed, the same exact location.

In ancient times, the Valley of Hinnom had a horrendous history. It had been used as a gathering place for pagan worshippers. All sorts of vile and wicked things, including burning children alive as sacrifices to the idols of Molach and Baal, occurred in that valley. One section of the valley was called Tophet, or the "fire-stove."[14] It was here where the children, mentioned in 2 Kings 23:10, were slaughtered.

What began as an ordinary fall morning in Jerusalem, ended in a re-fulfillment of scripture. On that morning, enemies of God tried to still the singing prayers of worshippers. As the day ended, there in the Valley of Hinnom, God's present-day army of worshippers fulfilled His word.

Sultan's Pool on Israeli Night.

Visiting with IDF soldiers on their base site
after sharing our dance program.

First-World Problems Versus A Third-World Reality

"But the Lord was with Joseph in the prison and showed him his faithful love."
Genesis 39:21

BEING OPEN TO the "beyond" in our lives requires commitment, endurance, surrender, and a deep humility that can only come from Christ. It requires faith to believe God is present and working in unseen ways when you are so ready to be released from your personal circumstances. This was especially true for me with two separate trips to third-world nations, Nigeria and Haiti.

I was invited to minister in Port Harcourt, Nigeria in January of 2016. The invitation was also extended to Stephanie Hall, a close friend and dance minister I have mentored. The assignment was to spend two weeks preparing a team of thirty-three Nigerians to lead in dance for an upcoming worship conference. Though I had been to South Africa several times, this was my first visit to Nigeria.

Nigeria is a country rich in hospitality, even though the poverty level is overwhelming. Nigerians have this gracious open quality when speaking that totally illuminates their faces. They simply smile as they speak. Song and dance are foundational elements of their culture, despite the impoverished surroundings.

Relationships are very important to me, and many lasting friendships have been formed during ministry engagements. There were several relationships during this trip that made a deep impact. Upon arrival in Port Harcourt we were taken to an enclosed and heavily guarded hotel compound. Needless to say, it was a bit daunting. I'm used to deplaning in foreign nations and being met by armed military forces, but these compound guards looked like plain-clothed pedestrians off the street. Stephanie and I never ventured out of the hotel for the entire week of training.

There was the initial meeting with the team and a bit of them sizing us up. What we wouldn't find out until later in the week was that for many of the students, this was the first time they had ever interfaced with teachers who were white skinned. Thankfully, this awkward phase only lasted one day. There is something about the love of God, when sincerely extended, that manages to dissolve walls of color. We began the amazing bonding experience by day two!

Evenings would bring a knock on the door from both the male and female members of the team. One of the beautiful qualities of the Nigerian culture is their regard and respect for elders and the strong belief in the passing of blessings from the older to the younger generations. Most of the requests from the team involved praying a blessing over them.

One young woman captured my heart. She was in her early twenties, smart, articulate, beautiful, bold, and passionate about her faith and the dreams she held in her heart. Desiring to enter governmental work, she wanted to make a difference in her sphere of influence. She had little to no financial provision or influence, but she was not going to allow her circumstances to steal her dreams. In our conversations, prayers, and spoken blessings, there was undeterred fire and a hope to be used by God as an agent of change. Considering those beautiful dark eyes, I was deeply moved by her passion.

Though loving the relational aspects of being in Nigeria, I was struggling with first-world problems in a third-world nation, namely personal comfort issues. I don't enjoy seeing bugs for which I have no name. I hate taking baths with a cereal bowl from a faucet that trickles water and sometimes stops flowing altogether. I dread electrical brownouts. Eating from only two food groups is hard on my digestive system, and not having 24/7 access to air-conditioning in 100 degree temperatures makes me cranky. I think I have painted the picture of life in many third-world nations. It continues to surprise me how much I take for granted living in America. Thankfully, in Nigeria we had water. But it is amid these uncomfortable conditions first-world dwellers feel as if they are incarcerated and want a "get out of jail free" card, now! And yet God is there with us, increasing our faith, endurance, and patience. These spiritual treasures are mined when we are void of choices.

First-world versus third-world collisions uncover pride. When pride issues are leveled, and we are surrendered, the atmosphere clears. Pride is a deep thick filter that colors attitudes, emotions, and decisions. In the Psalms, King David prayed, *"Let not the foot of pride come against me."* Why the metaphor of the foot? Feet leave heavy marks wherever they go. These imprints color every aspect of life. When humility is in the ascendancy, serving is distilled to simply loving.

Jeremiah 12:5 says," *If racing against mere men makes you tired, how will you race against horses? If you stumble and fall on open ground, what will you do in the thickets near the Jordan?"* During this time in Nigeria, any measure of strength, courage, or bravery to take these inconveniences in stride was being tested. And I was failing! My desire to be a horseman, an overcomer in this situation, led to a cry in prayer asking God for a strength beyond my own resources. As pride and discomfort took lesser roles, I began to see God's sovereignty working for purposes beyond my comfort level, purposes beyond cultural filters, purposes beyond my past experiences.

In my journal on January 7, 2016, I wrote these words as I heard them spoken by the Holy Spirit to my heart.

> *"So many things are transpiring you cannot see. These young ones who come to you for blessing have a destiny in Me. I have plans for their lives and a deposit for you to leave with them. Listen when I speak, and re-speak what I say to them. Rest in the knowledge you are here for Me. To represent Me. To speak My words. I will take care of you. Let not the enemy try to scare you. Stand firm and know I lead. Trust my words. Rest."*

I would be less, much less, than truthful if I did not tell you I wanted to kiss the ground upon returning to American soil. But I am thankful, grateful, and humbled to have been on this assignment. One of the treasures mined from this trip was a remark made by one of the young girls in our final meeting. When asked to share her experiences from our time together she said, *"I never knew I could be held and kissed by someone white."* There are no words to add for this gift.

Prior to Nigeria, a medical missions trip to Haiti ranked as number one in addressing my personal entitlement issues. Carl and I were together, and we traveled to a very remote village. There was no running water, no electricity, and many of the villagers had never seen white-skinned people. Our accommodations were not much more than glorified dog cages. The entire area where we were housed in the village was enclosed with a cyclone fence about twelve feet high. The rooms were three sided with no doors and no privacy. The villagers stood at the fence day and night just watching us. Around day two or three I wasn't sure I could handle feeling as if I was on display in the zoo. I remember thinking, "I can do this, but I need to get to the roof." I found a way to climb up on the roof and slept there each night for the remainder of the week. Just changing perspective and gaining a higher vantage point over the situation made all the difference. I was above it. I could breathe. Gaining my bearings, I could refocus and serve these people, which is why I was there.

There were other moments that almost did me in. The need in third-world nations is overwhelming. One of the most significant events of the Haiti trip came with partnering and assisting the medical triage team. Leaving the cyclone-fenced compound on one such venture to assess immediate needs, I met one of the women from the village. She invited me into her hut. It was made of mud and the floor was blackest earth. However, somehow she'd found some newspaper and papered the walls inside. She had also driven a wooden dowel into the mudded wall to hang her only pot. I am a bit of a decorator myself and was taken with her efforts to beautify her home. I was struck by the need for beauty God places in us. That desire to create a refuge for our families. To aspire to create beauty, even in the most impoverished settings, touched me deeply.

There were many selfish behaviors in Haiti that I was not proud of and wish I had the chance for a do-over! But if we remain engaged in this journey with the Lord, we do get the do-over! Saying "yes" to the purposes of God is not a one-time event. If we are truly going to be Christ-followers, then we need to be "yes" people. Retirement is a Western cultural concept. There is no retirement in God. Seasons change, ministry assignments are realigned, but saying "yes" to being used for His purposes remains, no matter how uncomfortable it makes you!

Like Esther in the Bible who used her influence to bring life to her people, we too can be life bearers, whether those people are in the streets of Nigeria, a village in Haiti, or in our local neighborhoods. Many times it is fear which stops us, such as the fear of venturing out of our comfort zones, fear of embarrassment, fear of danger, or fear of_____ (fill in your own blank). God willing, may we shut down fear and choose to bring good news along with the action required to implement the changes for transformation. Author Jeanne Damoff writes, "Fear is a fog that clouds the brain and freezes the heart."[15]

I would like to add to this by saying it is love in action that lifts the fog and ignites the heart.

My beautiful Nigerian students.

THE BEAUTY
BEHIND PRESSURE

"Let the godly sing for joy to the Lord; it is fitting for the pure to praise him. For the word of the Lord holds true and we can trust everything he does." Psalm 33:1–4

OUR GOD LOVES to uncover what is hidden to reveal unexpected treasure. There are many lessons to learn in the great "reveal." The discovery of tanzanite perfectly illustrates this point.

Legend has it during the 1960s lightning struck a field somewhere in Tanzania and caused the grasslands to catch fire.[16] Resident in this field were brown zoisite crystals on the surface of what appeared to be rocks. Under the intense heat of the fire, the rocks turned a brilliant blue. A group of tribesmen discovered this beautiful blue gem, now known as tanzanite. The tribesman who made the discovery thought the tanzanite stone had no value. Under the intense pressure of fire, what formerly had been hidden was suddenly and brilliantly revealed. What formerly had no value now had great worth because it was made beautiful under pressure. Today, the tanzanite gem is as valuable as diamonds!

To offer praise to God is to express our thanks, our love, and our respect simply because His essence, His nature, His ways, and His wisdom are good. In fact, they are perfect!

In life, offering praise is easy when we are happy, well, comfortable, and most of all, when we are in control. But life presents circumstances that aren't easy, happy, comfortable, or controlled. It is then our praise comes under pressure, and like hidden tanzanite, the pressure of circumstances serve to expose something in us—the invisible condition of our hearts. Whether we discover treasure or trash remains our choice.

A biblical example of praise under pressure is found in 2 Chronicles: 20. Word was rushed to King Jehoshaphat of Judah announcing the approach of a vast army. Knowing his own army was no match for the invading armies, Jehoshaphat turned to God for help and prayed. The entire prayer is worth the read, but one sentence in his prayer is riveting. *"We do not know what to do, but our eyes are upon You!"* Not knowing what to do, King Jehoshaphat made a choice to bow his knee and lift his voice in praise.

Is praising under pressure easy? It hasn't been for me. But, can God allow the pressure of our circumstance to create a treasure for Himself? Can He use the heat of fire in our soul to reveal a treasure in our hearts? Oh, absolutely yes!

Prior to a life of faith, I came face to face with a deep and dark depression. Self-medicating eased the pain sometimes, but the dark cloud loomed large when the escape ended. Dark visions and hallucinations were common during this time. During this dark period, I picked up a Bible I had been given as a high school graduation gift. Already in my late twenties, I had never opened it. In my desperation, I picked it up and began reading in the Psalms. I connected with the angst and deep cries of King David particularly in Psalm 6:6–7 when he cries, *"I am worn out from sobbing. All night I flood my bed with weeping, drenching it with my tears. My vision is blurred by grief."* I knew this experience well. I noticed also between the anguished cries of the psalmist, he would periodically declare, *"Praise the LORD."* After reading the Psalms night after night, I made a decision. I challenged myself upon waking to say out loud, *"I praise you LORD."* There was absolutely no emotion involved, no energy or conviction in the sound of my voice. I simply chose to speak this upon rising every morning. Months went by with no change.

I wish I could remember exactly how long I continued, but one day, on one of those mornings, the dark cloud over my mind and emotions began clearing. It was not long after I made a commitment to follow Christ. Like Jehoshaphat, I dared to praise before I saw the defeat of the darkness surrounding my emotions.

Reading the final chapter of 2 Chronicles chapter 20, we find Jehoshaphat went into the battle with praise and he came out of the victory with praise. He renamed the valley where the battle took place The Valley of Blessing. To praise God despite circumstances, because He is good, because He is worthy, because He is sovereign over all forces us to look up and out, not down and into ourselves. To praise under pressure is the choice we make before we know the results. This, dear reader, keeps our hearts healthy and our worship pure.

LIFE IN THE BELLY
OF THE WHALE

*"My eyes are straining to see your prom-
ises come true. When will you comfort
me? I am shriveled like a wineskin in the
smoke, but I have not forgotten to obey
your decrees. How long must I wait?"*
Psalm 119:82–84

THE BOOK OF Jonah is an interesting study of commitment and obedience under pressure. Jonah's fear and pride
caused him to choose disobedience and run from God. He
did not wish to go to Nineveh as God commanded, primarily because he was not convinced God would carry out
his threat to destroy the city. Instead, he boarded a ship
going in the opposite direction. A raging storm caused
the crew to cast lots, and it was determined Jonah was the
problem. They threw him overboard, and the scriptures say,
"God had already arranged for a great fish to swallow Jonah."

In the belly of the fish for three days and three nights, Jonah repented of his disobedience to God, and the fish spit him up on dry land. Listen to Jonah's prayer from the belly of the whale. *"Those who worship false gods turn their backs on all God's mercies. But I will offer sacrifices to you with songs of praise, and I will fulfill all my vows."* Jonah not only declared he would praise, but he would also "do!" He committed to return to Nineveh.

Commitment to wholehearted obedience is tested when we find ourselves in the "belly of the whale." Let me explain what I mean. You find yourself in a circumstance totally foreign; a place you have never been before, and through which you cannot find a way out! Added to the circumstance is an excruciating waiting period where you must hole up until a solution comes. You are at the mercy of God and God alone. Welcome to Jonah's world!

Nothing tests the commitment to obey like waiting. Waiting challenges our resolve and determination to hold steady in our love and loyalty to God. The year was 1999. The place was Washington, D.C. Although it is a distance from the coast, a whale managed to find me and swallow me up.

Carl and I had accepted a parachurch ministry position to pioneer a 24/7 worship and prayer house in the heart of the D.C. area. Carl would be part of the leadership team along with three others. I would lead the dance and worship arts aspect of the ministry. This was a huge move for us and entailed Carl leaving his position as chairman of development for a cataract teaching foundation, a position he had held for twenty years. I was an itinerate minister speaking and sharing in dance. Accepting this new assignment would put an end to all traveling. After much prayer, many questions, and discussions, we were offered a position with the ministry. Less than six months into the year the financial commitment made to us dried up and there was no remuneration. Carl and I had to move out of our rental home, went into thousands of dollars of debt, and our personal relationship as a married couple was fractured, to say the least. And yet, Carl had no release to leave before the year commitment was over.

To say this was possibly the worst year in our thirty-three-year marriage is an understatement! I like to think of myself as a peacemaker, not prone to angry outbursts. I had never experienced raw rage until that time! Being in the belly of a whale can reveal aspects of your nature you never knew existed. I was shocked to discover the Hulk and I had so much in common! I was angry, really angry, and I was not in control. One night while showering I started screaming, grabbing the shower curtain, and pulling it off the metal rod. I felt like a caged animal. Trapped, I was in the belly of the whale and didn't know how to get out. Please know, it was in this state of mind I went each evening to help lead worship and prayer. Can you imagine how effective my ministry before the Lord was during that time?

On one of these evenings I glanced over at the ministry leader, seething inside because in my heart I held him responsible for my misery. In that moment God spoke to my heart, *"He is my son."* I was shocked! Why didn't God agree with me? I had been maligned. Like Jonah, I had not factored in God's grace for "all" his sons and daughters. I was crying out for mercy, but it was tantamount for me to extend mercy.

Somehow I knew I wasn't getting out of this mess until I made a choice to release and bless the man. In obedience, and without an ounce of compassionate emotion, I walked over to him, blessed him with peace, and walked away. And with that, the whale spit me out!

Psalm 15:3–4 says one who does not keep his word and who slanders his neighbor cannot dwell in the presence of the Lord. I was guilty on both counts! Because of my disappointment with this leader, I wanted to break my word and leave, even if I didn't have a release to go. Because I felt I had suffered greatly and unjustly, I was angry, and I talked about it to anyone who would listen. Like Jonah, it took deep repentance and a renewed commitment to establish praise as a foundation in my life before entering the next season of ministry and life. Following the lessons learned in Washington, D.C., Carl and I relocated to Columbus, Ohio which turned out to be one of the richest seasons in our lives. It was in Columbus we were gifted with a beautiful community that became family. Our souls were restored and our hearts prepared for the final season of Carl's life.

GOD'S ESSENTIAL OILS

"... to give to them beauty for ashes, the oil of joy for mourning, the garment of praise for the spirit of heaviness." Isaiah 61:3

COSTLY PRAISE IS seen clearly in 2 Samuel 12:16–23. King David had committed adultery with Bathsheba and upon discovering she was pregnant, had her husband murdered. The prophet Nathan came to David with a parable revealing the secrets David had been hiding. As a judgment for this, the son born out of adultery was stricken with sickness and ultimately died. David begged God to spare the child. He went without food and lay all night on the bare ground.

"Then on the seventh day the child died. David's advisers were afraid to tell him. He wouldn't listen to reason while the child was ill, they said. What drastic thing will he do when we tell him the child is dead? When David saw them whispering, he realized what had happened.

Is the child dead? he asked. Yes, they replied, he is dead."

The passage goes on to say David got up from the ground, bathed, anointed himself with oil, changed his clothes, and went to the Tabernacle to worship the Lord. Afterward, he returned to the palace and was served food and ate.

In his grief David chose to move forward. He began the first steps of moving past his pain. When we are suffering deep pain, especially loss, our praise is very costly in the sight of God. It takes every drop of energy to make yourself move forward. It requires stamina and exertion to remain thankful. To praise, in the midst of sorrow, is a costly sacrifice.

To love deeply is to risk hurt and pain, but David's example teaches a powerful truth regarding moving past loss. First, we must leave the results of disappointment in God's hands and trust His sovereign choices for our lives. I do not want to minimize the difficulty of disappointment and grief. It is all too real as I know from experience, but we must willfully decide to get up from our bed of grief, anoint ourselves with oil, and get into the presence of God.

Carl lost his battle with cancer in 2012. One of the most difficult times of walking through the fight for his life occurred during a two-week trip we made to Mexico for experimental medical treatments.

Carl was weak and oh, so sick. Traveling from Ohio to Mexico had taken a toll on us, and the arrangements in the hospital were difficult. Carl had his own private room, but I was required to sleep on another floor of the hospital in one of the vacant hospital beds. After making sure Carl was settled and almost asleep, I would take the elevator to my hospital bed in the sterile environment of the fourth floor. Nights were the worst.

On one of the mornings of Carl's treatment, I stayed in my room. I was at a loss how to communicate the depth of despair and sorrow I was experiencing so I went to prayer with my second language, dance.

I sensed the Holy Spirit urging me to move as I spoke this scripture from Psalm 118:24: *"This is the day the Lord has made, I will rejoice and be glad in it."*

On that morning I danced tearfully, not beautifully. I danced simply, not creatively. In my sorrow, it took every ounce of strength and will to offer this costly sacrifice.

Studying the scriptures for a teaching a few years later, I saw a metaphorical picture of three spiritual oils. I believe these spiritual examples contribute to the DNA of a worshipper. The oil of suffering is the first example of these oils and is illustrated in the garden scene of Luke 22:41. What is translated as Gethsemane comes from two Hebrew words, *gat* and *shmanim.*[17] Its meaning is "the place where olive oil is pressed." The pressure needed to extract oil from olives is extremely intense. The circumstances where we experience the pressure of pain so strongly we do not feel we can bear it becomes our Gethsemane. But it is here, despite the pain, we choose God's will, God's choice, what will bring God's greatest glory.

Please know when you are hurting this deeply and simply want the pain to go away you are in good company. Even Jesus asked three times, *"if it were possible,"* the cup of suffering would be taken from Him. Nevertheless, He chose God's will.

The second costly spiritual oil is found in Isaiah 61:3: *"... to give to them beauty for ashes, the oil of joy for mourning, the garment of praise for the spirit of heaviness; that they might be called trees of righteousness, the planting of the Lord, that he might be glorified."*

Mourning is the result of loss, not only the death of a loved one, but with each season of life. Sometimes the loss is precipitated by changing relationships, health, finances, or employment. The list goes on and on. Difficult seasons of life make joy seem intangible; we wonder if joy will ever return. But we are promised the supply of the oil of joy will always be available. Joy will not run out; it will come again. It is assured for those who suffer loss. Nothing is as sweet as the taste of joy after much sorrow. While it may seem slow in coming, we have the promise it will be given after the mourning season is over.

The third spiritual oil is the oil of intimacy. In Matthew 25:2–4, we have the story of the ten virgins: *"Five of them were wise, and five were foolish. Those who were foolish took their lamps and took no oil with them, but the wise took oil in their vessels with their lamps."*

The oil of intimacy represents the presence of the Holy Spirit in our lives. Developing an intimate relationship with the third person of the godhead is costly. It requires a surrendered heart and time spent in His presence. In addition, there is also the cultivating of obedience that comes with such intimacy. The fragrance of Christ emanates from worship amid suffering, joy emerging from mourning, and obedience rising from the depths of intimacy. We begin to smell like Him! Habakkuk 3:17 says it best: *"Even though the fig trees have no blossoms and there are no grapes on the vine; even though the olive crop fails and the fields lie empty and barren; even though the flocks die in the field and the cattle barns are empty, yet I will rejoice in the LORD! I will be joyful in the God of my salvation. The Sovereign LORD is my strength. He will make me as surefooted as a deer and bring me safely over the mountains."*

Embracing the costly sacrifice of praise strengthens us and the pressure from the crucible of difficult circumstances yields a lasting treasure in the sight of God.

Celebrating a landmark anniversary in Italy
a few years before Carl's diagnosis.

THE GERALD MCBOING BOING SYNDROME

"He forever made perfect those who are being made holy." Hebrews 10:14

ONE OF MY favorite books as a child was *Gerald McBoing Boing*, authored by Dr. Seuss in 1950.[18] This story seemed to articulate my childhood insecurities of feeling like a misfit in my family. Let me clarify here. I in no way was unloved or abused by my parents or siblings. However, I wasn't quite like any of them, either. Being the middle child, I wasn't the rule follower like my elder sister, and I didn't enjoy the baby status like my younger one. I might mention I wasn't as compliant as either one of them either. I grew up feeling terribly misunderstood and sort of forged my own path, but not without a great deal of inner childhood angst. In a casual conversation with my daughter Zana, I mentioned my desire to find a copy of the *McBoing Boing* book, and so like Zana, she secured a copy and gifted it to me a few weeks later!

One of the lesser known books by Dr. Seuss, the main character is properly named Gerald McCloy who at age two when most kids start talking "went BOING BOING instead." As a misfit and a disappointment to his parents, his vocabulary didn't change but increased to sounds like BOOM, HONK, and CUCKOO. Gerald's lack of words and increased use of sounds made him an embarrassment to his family and alienated him from his peers in school.

While I never spoke nonsensical words in lieu of conversation, my ideas, my imaginary play, and my dreams all seemed at odds with the traditional expectations of the "normal" that surrounded me. It's a curious thing when you write about your past. As a writer you want to be honest, vulnerable, and at all costs refrain from rewriting history. My mother is gone now, so unfortunately I can't include her perspective. It was, however, my child's worldview that because I was not "like" my sisters, I was much more difficult to deal with. If I were to fit in I needed to work hard at finding out who people wanted me to be and performing well to get there. Acceptance-based performance remained my chameleon mode of operation for a good part of my adult years.

Returning to the story of *Gerald McBoing Boing*, poor Gerald, unable to take the pain of rejection any longer, decided to run away from home. But miracle of miracles, he is found by a kind and famous owner of the BONG-BONG-BONG Radio Station. Gerald, it seems, was just what he was looking for, a radio personality who could make multiple sounds for characters and animals on the show. Gerald became well known, well fed, prosperous, and famous. And finally, his parents were proud of him.

How I loved the resolution. All his oddities and quirks were validated. Gerald was finally accepted just as he was created. It took the radio station owner to recognize and call out his gifting, but he was vindicated and rewarded.

Parents are made proud by the accomplishments of their children primarily because it reflects well on them. It's a "humankind" reaction to the success of one you have been instrumental in molding. But beyond parental and peer approval is the unchanging, unconditional, unreserved love of God for His creation—you! In all your quirky oddities, you are His divine workmanship.

We do not have to perform to receive God's love. In fact, we need to guard our devotion from becoming a matter of works rather than a response from a heart of love. If we come to God with only a list of wants and needs, we relegate the Holy One of all creation to a spiritual vending machine. If we come with a litany of prepackaged prayers and devotional readings that need to be moved through quickly so we can go on with our day, then our love for God is reduced to a task, not a connection. Without connectedness, without engaging the heart, without a listening ear for what God might speak, we are little better than bad performers. To finally recognize we are totally, unequivocally loved by God is freedom's greatest reward. Gerald McBoing Boing's rejection of his uniqueness caused him to run away. Dear reader, what might you be running from that is uniquely part and parcel of the divine DNA God placed in you?

Hebrews 10:14 says, *"For by one offering [Jesus Christ], he forever made perfect those who are being made holy."* Followers of Christ are forever made perfect! Jesus' sacrifice on the cross as a sin offering forever made us perfect in the Father's eyes. There is no performance, no jumping through fire hoops to secure a more solid standing. We are, however, in the process of being made holy. In other words, perfect but still in process! Thank you, Dr. Seuss and Gerald McBoing Boing for somehow giving me permission to accept who I was at six years old even though I continued to struggle with performance-based acceptance for another five decades.

While I am better at having accepted God's unconditional love for me in this season of my life, I continue to
struggle with "doing" as opposed to "being." To rest without
the need to produce remains a battle of engagement. A most
recent journal entry from my time with the Lord:

> *"Don't confuse love with purpose. My purpose
> leads you to fullness of life. My love is uncon-
> ditionally anchored in me and my care for
> you. If you never leave your sofa I cannot love
> you less."*

We so seldom meet people who deeply know the unconditional love of God. Without experiential knowledge of
this freedom we have difficulty releasing it to others. When
we find one of these extravagant lovers, we want them as
friends for life. Oh, that we could be more like the kind
owner of BONG-BONG-BONG Radio Station calling
out gifting and seeing potential and greatness in others.

BE WHAT YOU IS!

*"For the dead cannot praise you; they cannot
raise their voices in praise. Those who go
down to the grave can no longer hope in your
faithfulness." Isaiah 38:18*

THE LOSS OF the living presence of someone you love
deeply is only known by the bereaved. There are few words
to describe the emptiness. The cavernous darkness disori-
ents you emotionally and leaves so few words to articulate
the new normal without them. Worship is the balm that
heals, but moving "through" the "valley of the shadow of
death" is a challenge. Nothing in my walk with the Lord has
tested my heart of worship more than losing Carl.

During his first hospitalization in April of 2011, before
we had a diagnosis as to what was going on, I was scheduled to teach in our home church. Carl was recovering from
having a thoracentesis procedure, which removes fluid from
the space between the lungs and chest wall. He was adamant
about being in the service on Sunday. He came early and

went straight up to the sound booth to avoid any hugs that might aggravate the port site. I can still see his face watching me as I taught.

The text for my teaching was based on Ecclesiastes 3: *"In everything there is a season, a time for every purpose under heaven."* The emphasis of my message was verse eight, *"A time of war."* Little did I know waiting for me on the horizon was a personal war with suffering and a raging battle of sorrow. Over the next two years verses such as, *"A time to love, a time to weep, a time to mourn, and a time to die"* would take the ascendancy.

In reviewing my notes from this sermon in 2011, I am not sure I included the following quote by Tertullian, but my rough draft notes ended with it. Tertullian lived around 200 AD. Highly educated, he was a product of his culture and attended the games where gladiators killed for the pleasure of the spectators. At those games, he witnessed Christians being executed in this manner reacting differently. He witnessed slaves with great courage facing this horrid and hideous death. After investigating these Christians, he came to faith. Tertullian, through his writings, became an apologist for the cause of Christ. He wrote, *"The Lord challenges us to suffer persecutions and to confess him. He wants those who belong to him to be brave and fearless. He himself shows how weakness of the flesh is overcome by courage of the Spirit. This is the testimony of the apostles. A Christian is fearless."*[19] I hungered for these noble words attesting to great character. It was quite a different matter to digest them!

Why do suffering and death knock us down so readily and why do we have so many questions when they come? As Christ-followers we agree with Romans 8:29 that *"we are predestined to be conformed into the image of Christ Jesus."* We attest to Luke 6:40 that *"a student is not above the teacher and everyone fully trained will be like their teacher."* We support Hebrews 5:8, which says, *"Even though Jesus was God's son, he learned obedience from the things He suffered."* And we choose to acknowledge according to Romans 8:17: *"We share in the glory of God as children of God . . . only if we share in His sufferings."* But when these truths come to us and require implementation, oh my, that is when the proverbial "rubber meets the road!"

We are designed and equipped by God to "walk through" the darkness of suffering, but sometimes the process of walking through the darkness causes the darkness to lodge inside of us, and the darkness we were created to walk through instead begins to shape and define us. I had a theology of worship, but I did not have a theology for suffering. We need both to navigate the darkness.

Theology simply means to study God's truth on a subject. I did not realize I would need a theology for suffering prior to the situation I would experience with Carl. My theology of suffering is not brilliant, conclusive, or totally encompassing. It was formed from my "in the trenches" journey of suffering with Carl through the last two years of his life and my grief following his loss.

Suffering produces pain, and pain hurts. Not a brilliant statement, but certainly not understood in its fullness until deep pain has come to you. You cannot always see cancer. You cannot always perceive mental and emotional illness or the grief that brings such suffering to the ones who bear it. You cannot always know the pain and anguish of those who must watch afflicted ones suffer. Total helplessness is one of the phrases that come to mind! I remember one such time with Carl.

It was early in the diagnosis, and we decided to leave Ohio and return to Florida for an extended visit. My parent's homestead was vacant due to having moved them into an Alzheimer's facility a year prior. The furnishings in Florida were sparse, but we were with family and, of course, the grandchildren. During one of the first evenings after arriving, Carl and I were in bed and, as usual, he fell asleep first. As I listened to his breathing, which was not labored at that time but certainly more rapid than it had ever been, I tried to match my breathing rhythm to his. It was then I realized how many times he had to inhale to get air to his lungs. This all transpired around 2:00 AM. I engaged in this exercise for about five minutes and could stand it no longer. I got up from the bed, went to the living room, and simply began to sob. I could barely stand the thought of his impairment. Carl must have heard me and came into the living room. He stood in the doorway and asked what was the matter. Through sobs and tears I told him what I had done while lying next to him. You would have to know Carl to understand his quirky wit and seamless timing to understand what he said next. At two-something in the morning, awakened from sound sleep by the sobbing of his wife, Carl looked at me and said, "Yvonne, be what you is, and not what you is not!" And with that, he turned around and went back to sleep.

The obscure quote comes from a program that debuted on NBC in October of 1960 and ran for over a year.[20] The character Tudor Turtle, through the help of Mr. Wizard's magic, could alter his destiny by going back in time. This would inevitably turn into a disaster, and Tudor would cry out, "Help me Mr. Wizard, I don't want to be—anymore!"—would be whatever destiny Tudor had entered. Mr. Wizard would bring Tudor back to reality with this incantation: "Twizzle, Twaddle, Twozzle, Twome; time for this one to come home." Mr. Wizard would then give this advice to Tudor: "Be just what you is, not what you is not. Folks what do this has the happiest lot." Only Carl could remember and retrieve this from his Rolodex file of memories. He was amazing in that way. I was shocked! I did stop crying and eventually went back to bed. While Carl's sense of humor defused my grief for the night, I knew I needed greater trust in God for His grace in Carl's life; but I also needed to find the greater grace necessary for my journey as well.

For the first steps of this new normal I revisited the steps of an ancient path traveled by Jesus. His experience in the Garden of Gethsemane. I have cried myself sick begging for mercy on Carl's behalf. I have wanted to die knowing we are separated. I have felt the agonizing sorrow of deep grief, but I have never bled through my pores. While this fact did not keep me from my own ache, it demanded I look at Jesus and consider His experience. And when I did, I realized I was not alone in my pain.

The name *Gethsemane*, as I have already stated, is a corruption into English of two Hebrew words *gat* and *shamanim*.[21] At an ancient olive press, the olives would have been gathered into sacks and stacked one on top of another. A beam would then be lowered onto the stack and increasing weight added to the end of the beam to press oil from the olives. The more pressure, the more oil! Similarly, by process, grapes are crushed and undergo pressure to be made into wine. Both olives and grapes are literally "squeezed to death" to be made a product for consumption. God uses the uncomfortable processes of weight, pressure, and squeezing in the "Gat Shamanims" of our lives to fashion the threads of our tapestry. Our surrendered tapestry in the hands of the Master Weaver is then used to bring comfort to help fashion others.

The setting of Gethsemane with its imagery of pressure and suffering spoke to me. Cries from Matthew 26 such as, *"My heart is so filled with sadness that I could die!* and *"My Father, if possible, let this cup pass from me!"* aptly articulated my groaning. In these verses alone, I saw Jesus suffering the same kind of anguish I was experiencing. I saw Jesus, knowing the Father could do the impossible, pleading if there was any way for this situation to pass or have a different outcome, then to please remove it. That is exactly how I felt! In John 18:11, however, I also saw Jesus' acceptance and trust in embracing the Father's will when he said, *"This is the cup the Father has given me; am I not to drink it?"* While I was not at the acceptance stage, I knew at the very least Jesus understood what I was experiencing. It was a hard comfort, but it was comfort nonetheless.

Our American culture is not conducive to these raw kingdom principles and reality. It is an affront to our comfort zones, entitlement, and pleasure-seeking ways. But according to Paul in Romans 8:16, *"The Spirit himself bears witness with our own spirit that we are children of God; and if we are children, then we are also heirs, heirs of God and joint heirs with the Messiah—provided we are suffering with him in order also to be glorified with him."* He goes on to say that these *"sufferings we are going through now are not even worth comparing with the glory that will be revealed to us in the future."* Identifying with Jesus, being a follower of Christ in this life means we are not immune to sickness, suffering, and death. Suffering wasn't what happened to Paul or to people in other nations. Suffering had come to me. This was hard fact! But, I was sensing His companionship in the suffering, and that was a comforting reality.

Does suffering for the sake of suffering make God's heart glad? Absolutely not! Lamentations 3:33 clearly says, *"For he does not willingly bring affliction or grief to anyone."* But in our suffering, by choosing trust in His sovereign care and goodness, can suffering bring forth transformation? Assuredly yes! 2 Corinthians 1:3–4 speaks of the weight of troubles and a God who comforts amid them. *"[It is God] who comforts us in all our troubles."* How interesting that the word for "trouble" has the meaning of pressing and great pressure. And so, it is God who comforts us during our "winepress of oils" in order that we comfort others in theirs. In Jesus, we have a Savior who gave His life in the pressure cooker of Gethsemane as a supreme sacrifice for us. We have a Savior who joins us in our suffering, and we have a Savior who takes us from this life into an eternity with no more suffering.

Mr. Wizard couldn't change my destiny, but Jesus could see me through it.

Gift from Carl: No date

I found this scrap of paper tucked away in your Bible when packing for my move to Florida.

"If we live in the sorrow of the past, which we cannot change, we will grow very little in the life and truth that Jesus offers."

A CHANGE OF PERSPECTIVE

"But as for me, how good it is to be near God!
I have made the Sovereign LORD my shelter,
and I will tell everyone about the wonderful
things you do." Psalm 73:28

OUR NEARNESS TO God changes our perspective.
There is an antiquated word used in medical settings. The
word is *incarn* and describes the flesh that grows over a
wound.[22] Applied to healing, incarn refers to the recovery
of wounded flesh due to the presence of new flesh. Because
of the incarnation of Christ coming in the flesh, He enters
our suffering and covers our wounds by His Spirit; and that
changes everything. Suffering still hurts, but Jesus brings
with Him the balm necessary to heal wounds. These wounds
are not limited to sin alone, but also emanate from the suffering of broken hearts and troubled minds. As we draw
near and allow Him to cover our wounds, we are healed;
we are changed. Whether from divorce, a broken heart, a
troubled mind, or loss of a loved one, the open wound is

incarned with the Spirit of God bringing new flesh, His flesh, and we begin to heal.

Craig Scott penned this quote: "From every wound there is a scar, and every scar tells a story. A story that says, I survived."[23] Jesus was wounded and bears scars. Those scars tell a story. In His story, we not only survive, but are destined to live forever in an eternity without pain, death, or scars.

Mothers who have birthed children will understand this analogy. During birth pains, there is no option but to go through. You can't say, "Hey, not really wanting to do this now, let me come back in a few days and we will try again." Funny story! I had a friend who wanted to be a great witness for Christ in the labor room when she went to have her first baby. As I remember her telling the story all went well until the last stages of hard labor. At that point, her witness was a screaming exclamation, "JESUS, GET THIS BABY OUT OF ME!" When it is time to birth there is no turning back. And so it is when God uses suffering to birth purpose.

When Jesus was about to depart earth, He knew those who loved Him would suffer and grieve. Here is what He said to them in John 16:20: "*. . . you will weep and mourn . . . you will grieve, but your grief will be turned to joy. A woman giving birth to a child has pain . . . but when her baby is born, she forgets the anguish, because of her joy that a child is born* *into the world."* Jesus does not deny the process and pain, but He promises a return to joy.

I love the raw truth God reveals in His Word. From Psalm to Psalm we get a realistic perspective of suffering. Psalm 9:9 wonderfully declares, *"You are a refuge in times of trouble."* Psalm 10:1, however screams, *"Why are you so far off in the time of trouble."* Psalm 20:1 softly declares, *"The Lord hear you in your time of trouble."* Psalm 25:14 passionately cries out, *"The sorrow of my heart is so enlarged, bring me out of my distress."* Whether confidently declaring His word and promises or in anguished grief crying out in pain, our choice and source are still the God of all creation! And whether sweetly spoken or bitterly groaned, God hears and answers.

We enjoy His promises in good times, but we must wrestle and cling to them in the sad and challenging seasons. When we are happy, there is little engagement of our will. Trust seems to flow. When we are suffering, the flow of trust slows down, stagnates, and even solidifies. It is then we must choose to trust God's sovereign purpose. The alternate choices are retreating, rebelling, or resenting the purpose. God's enduring promises are true, tried, and tested. The voices battling our mind from an army of doubt seek to cast shadows on those promises during a season of suffering.

By an act of our will we must consider God's faithful past and surrender afresh to what He plans for our future.

One of the primary ways to keep the flow of trust from stagnating is worship. In worship, we "will" to give God thanks, praise, and glory simply because He is God and He is good. How does worship look in the environs of deep darkness? Let me tell you, it is not particularly pretty and certainly is rawer and less polished.

I would like to share an entry from my journal as I observed Carl one morning.

According to Romans 12, we are to present our bodies as a living sacrifice. This constitutes a holy and acceptable spiritual service to God. Today, as I watch Carl worship, suffering through weakened movement of his skeletal frame, catching the image of visible-tumors poking through his T-shirt, fitful coughing. I ask myself how this image fulfills this scripture? The answer is found in verse two. The outward appearance of the offering is not the essence of acceptance. It is the transformation by the renewing of our mind that helps us think like God, and agree with Him for what is perfect, pleasing, and good. It is the transformed mind that will prove the good and acceptable and perfect will of God in our lives and not the polished outward appearance. Suffering does not excuse us from the substance of offering. Perhaps that is why it is called a sacrifice. But transformation through a renewed mind will bring us into agreement with what God deems perfect and good.

In the Old Testament Job comes to mind as a major player in suffering. Though, at the end of his dark night he was blessed with 14,000 sheep, 6,000 camels, 1,000 yoke of oxen, 1,000 donkeys, 7 sons and 3 daughters, and another 140 years of life, his greatest reward is found near the end of the book. Chapter 42 is preceded by four chapters of grueling questions God asked of Job. The questions began with, *"Where were you when I laid the earth's foundation? Tell me if you understand,"* and didn't end until pages later. When Job could respond, he says this, *"I know that you can do all things; no purpose of yours can be thwarted. Surely, I spoke of things I did not understand, things too wonderful for me to know. My ears had heard of you, but now my eyes have seen you, therefore I despise myself and repent in dust and ashes."* Job came into his "Be who you is and not who you is not" moment!

Suffering births purpose, but many times the purpose is hidden and known only to God and more than likely must wait until eternity to be revealed. Nothing can thwart His purpose, and no amount of prideful speculation can help explain it. Just ask Job's three friends. Changing our perspective helps us see a new and different purpose, purpose pregnant with hope and a future. Jeremiah speaks about this hope in chapter 29:11: *"For I know the plans I have for you, declares the Lord, plans to prosper you and not to harm you, plans to give you a hope and a future."* There is no hope without a secure future, and the future is frightening without hope. Only God is big enough to bring the two—hope and a future—together for His purpose. The beautiful poem from Ecclesiastes says, *"In everything there is a season, a time for every purpose under heaven."* All seasons whether good or bad, fun or difficult, comfortable or disastrous, are only for a season. Whatever season you find yourself in, dear reader, choose the way of trust.

EYE OF THE NEEDLE

"I will speak to you in parables and explain
mysteries from days of old." Psalm 78:2

THERE ARE AT least three generally accepted inter-
pretations in Matthew 19:24 when Jesus said, *"It is easier*
to go through the eye of a needle than for a rich person to
enter the Kingdom of God."[24] One school of thought refers
to an ancient Persian expression of impossibility stating it
would be easier for an elephant to go through the eye of a
needle, than for whatever was the impossibility of the situation. The camel then was an adaptation since camels were
the biggest animals around Israel.

A second explanation was a possible mix-up of the
Greek word for "camel," *kamelos,* and the word for "cable,"
kamilos. It would then make sense for the impossibility of a
cable, rather than a camel, to go through the eye of a needle.

A third, and final theory is the possibility of an actual
gate in Jerusalem that was literally a gate within a gate.
When the larger gate was closed at night for security reasons,

the inner gate, called the eye of the needle, would be opened. After dark, merchants and camels loaded with wares would come into the city via this gate. The camels would have to be stripped of all they carried to crawl through the smaller opening. The problem with this theory is there is no impartial evidence to suggest such a gate existed.

I lay out this information because I desire you, my reader, to know it is not my intent to engage in theology here. Clearly the context of Jesus' hyperbole was regarding the inability of man to procure his own salvation regardless of rank or possessions. What I want to share is a prophetic parable given by Dr. E. Charlotte Baker at the 1981 National Worship Symposium in Dallas, Texas.[25] The entire parable was unplanned, unwritten, unrehearsed, and spoken spontaneously on one of the evenings of the conference.

Using the imagery of the eye of the needle as being a small gate, the parable utilizes the hyperbolic concept of this gate as a point of entry, one necessary to crawl through if one desires to be a worshipper of God. The main character asks for different gifts along his journey. The first gifting he asks for is artistry in the ability to play an instrument and sing in the house of the Lord. Through this gifting, he desires to do great exploits for God. The request is granted, and the expression of gifting moved "the hearts of men." But something remained unsatisfied. There was an ache for more. The parable continues with the asking for healing gifts to relieve suffering and pain in the nations. Gifts of power to pierce the powers of darkness were requested. Each time the main character requests and is granted grace-filled gifts, he returns with more longing. And so, the parable ultimately moves to an invitation from God to come up higher in the spiritual realm and see what is happening from a heavenly perspective. It is there our "son of man" sees many gathered around a small gate called the eye of the needle. From this perspective, he can see many gifted lovers of God unwilling to release their gifts to crawl through the very narrow gate. He is the only one who releases all his gifts, and after going low, very low, he finds all the gifts he released waiting on the other side.

Parables themselves have been widely used in literature and in both Old and New Testaments. Jesus' use of the parable to teach kingdom truths has no parallel. Dr. Baker's parable, designed to illustrate a rich truth of worship, shaped my understanding as a worshipper of God. Although I did not attend the National Worship Symposium in 1981, my good friend, songwriter and international worship leader Kirk Dearman, was present. He accompanied Dr. Baker on the piano by undergirding the narrative with instrumental music. I have asked him in his own words to share his experience.

That final night of the worship symposium is one that will stand out as one the greatest spiritual highlights of my life. The conference attendees were all seated at a long banquet table and we had just enjoyed a wonderful meal in the VIP guest "box seat" suite, high at the top floor of the former Texas Stadium. As we entered a time of worship and waiting on the Lord, the manifest presence and glory of the Lord fell upon us all in a usually strong way. At one point, His majestic presence was so palpable and overwhelming that a 'holy hush' fell over the room; we began to kneel or to lay prostrate before Him, in silent reverence and awe. I can honestly say I had never before—or since—been more aware of God's awesome presence. His glory was truly passing by us all, and we could only respond in astonished wonder. Some were softly weeping; others were quietly singing in the Spirit. Charlotte rose from her chair and slowly made her way to the center of the room. Pastor Olen Griffing, then senior pastor of Shady Grove Church, in Grand Prairie— my pastor at that time—motioned for me to move to the piano. As I began to softly play, Charlotte began to prophesy. I have never— or since—heard a prophesy come forth as an allegory. It was delivered so perfectly. It was as if she had previously written it. I learned later that prophetic allegories were one of Charlotte's spiritual gifts, and it was truly something to behold.

The worship dancers began to move out, spontaneously interpreting the allegory, while I provided spontaneous musical underscoring. But the presence of the Lord was so strong, I could hardly sit at the piano. I just wanted to be prostrated before Him. When Charlotte finally ceased to prophesy, everyone was weeping, and a spirit of deep repentance had filled the room. The Lord was humbling us all and was clearly calling us to 'go lower still' and to lay aside our artistic gifts at the portal to the eye of the needle, in order that we might go through it and–in His timing— emerge as vessels of honor, taking up those gifts in the power of the Holy Spirit and be used for His glory in ever-increasing measure.

> *For me personally, the fulfillment of the eye*
> *of the needle prophetic allegory has been an*
> *ongoing and often painful process, and it has*
> *taken a lifetime. My constant prayer is that*
> *the Lord would change me into a vessel of*
> *honor for Him and be mightily used in what-*
> *ever way He chooses.*

In this beautifully articulated parable, a kernel of true love is revealed. This small gate is the gate of worship. The Colossians 1:16 text says, *"All things were created by him and for him. He is before all things and in him all things hold together. In everything he has the supremacy."* Gifts are a pleasure to receive, but they are just that, gifts, given from the hand of the Gift Giver. Therefore, what is greater, the gift or the gift giver? In our humanity, our gifts can become idols. In humility, our worship is centered on the One from whom all blessings emanate. All our gifts come from His hand and for this, worship is due His name.

The parable has been translated in both Portuguese and Spanish, and I have choreographed the allegory presenting it to audiences throughout the world. Many other Christian artists and friends have ministered these words as well. The parable is a valuable reminder from the Romans 11:36 doxology: *"For from him and through him and for him are all things. To him be the glory forever! Amen."* All gifting comes from the hand of God. The book of Romans states we have all been given gifts. The gifts are given that we might bring glory to the God who gave them.

In our humanness, we desire, grasp, and feel a tremendous need to be affirmed by purpose, to find our identity in what we can do, what we can acquire, what defines us. "The Eye of the Needle" allegory speaks again the question asked in the Westminster Catechism, "What is the chief end of man?"[26] The answer? "Man's chief end is to glorify God, and to enjoy him forever." Nowhere has this truth been more evident than in my journey as a worshipper. My worship expression was formed through dance, but my life's pursuit has extended well beyond the dance for a desire to know God.

I had the distinct honor of being mentored by Charlotte. I remember one time speaking to her backstage at a conference where we both happened to be guest ministers. I was bemoaning my personal desire to experience a deeper relationship with the Lord and being surrounded by many who had no desire to explore the depths of God. Charlotte looked deeply into my eyes and said, "Yvonne, not everyone wants to fly." I remember being taken aback by her words. Maturity and experience have taught me timing is everything, judging others is deadly, and I didn't know then as much as I thought I did! Yes, I still want to fly like the eagle. Yes, the pursuit of God and the elimination of distractions make the journey a little lonely at times. Certainly, I have been misunderstood, but I choose to be a worshipper. I choose the narrow gate. I treasure a signed copy of Charlotte's book. In it she wrote, "God bless you, Yvonne. Keep flying where the eagle flies!" Dr. Charlotte E. Baker has entered her eternal reward. It was with extreme honor I could choreograph "Eye of the Needle" for her memorial service and dance it with several artists who were impacted by her life.

Oh reader, may you aspire to love and trust your Creator, and believe for the courage and strength to fly high!

> *"But those who trust in the Lord will find new strength. They will soar high on wings like eagles. They will run and not grow weary. They will walk and not faint."* (Isaiah 40:31)

Gift to Carl: 2012

Your last wish, on your last Christmas on earth, was watermelon. I kept trying to explain to you as you lay in the Meleck Hospice House, room #15, Autumn Wing, that it was Christmas Day. The stores were closed. Publix was not open! I'm not sure you understood because you kept asking for watermelon, nonetheless. You were always so determined, so tenacious when you wanted something. That quality, in fact, is how you won my heart. I was desperate to find watermelon for you on Christmas Day. The hospice house had a small kitchen for the workers. There was a refrigerator in the room. I opened it and found a fruit salad someone had purchased for their dinner. I am unashamed to say I stole "only" the watermelon from the prepackaged salad bowl. Thankfully I could give you what you wanted for Christmas. I would do it again!

THE "CARL" FACTOR

"They are confident and fearless and can face their foes triumphantly. They share freely and give generously to those in need. Their good deeds will be remembered forever. They will have influence and honor." Psalm 112:8–9

THIS CHAPTER IS probably one of the most difficult to pen. It comes out of a dry spell in working to complete this manuscript. A recent event made it clear to me why the delay was necessary. Something had to take place before this chapter could be written.

Beyond the Dance is dedicated to Carl for several reasons. While God is the author of my life, Carl is the writer God used to bring my story to life. I'm quite sure had Carl not spoken to me at the camera counter during that fateful late December, my story might have had a different plot. Carl believed in me. He supported and called out gifting he saw in me. He selflessly pushed me to pursue God's purpose and planned destiny for my life.

In the past few days through a series of circumstances, Michael, a family member, was admitted to a hospice facility. I quickly discovered it was the same one Carl was admitted to four years prior. Driving into the parking lot I had to pause and collect myself. Meeting my sister Diana there, I walked to room #15 of Autumn Wing. I had a sense I was headed to the same room where Carl took his last breath. As soon as I rounded the corner of the nurse's station I knew! I was returning to a former chapter in my story.

December 25, 2012, was the first time I crossed the threshold to room #15. I remember the exact moment I walked into the room with Carl. Written over the window in stenciled letters was the word HOPE. I would desperately cling to that word for the next three days. And now, four years, minus forty-four days, HOPE again greeted me as I walked into the room.

Because my sister was exhausted, I offered to spend the night with Michael. Emotionally I felt fine. My mind was recalling memories, but I felt in control. Around 9:00 PM the night nurse came in to check on us. She sat down, and we begin to chat. Michael was nonresponsive and I was telling her about his life and the obstacles he had overcome. Previously, my brother-in-law mentioned to the nurse Carl had been in this very room.

From the moment I walked into room #15 I had the sense there was a purpose for being there. It seemed too random not to be divine. I mentioned this to the night nurse. In further conversation I found myself telling her Carl and I were never able to say goodbye to each other. Somehow, we couldn't find the words. With that comment, she looked me straight in the eyes and said, "This is why you are here. Until you say goodbye, you can't go on!" I was undone! I began to cry and realized God had orchestrated this moment. One more layer of healing albeit four years later. I can't begin to tell you, dear reader, why it took me four years to say goodbye to Carl. But in that moment something began to shift emotionally. I felt lighter.

I have shared the story of how Carl and I met as well as the challenges of living and dying with cancer. However, I wanted to share a few glimpses into Carl's personality in the in-between years. Our lives are impacted, shaped, and sharpened by those whom we join during our lifetimes. Being married to Carl was a transforming experience!

Carl's sense of humor was quirky and corny. He either made me laugh until I cried, or roll my eyes and grown, "Oh, Carl!" Carl had this effect on all those who knew him, I might add. One of his closest friends, Scott Osborne, presided over Carl's memorial service. Scott knew Carl well and had experienced a few of those, "Oh, Carl!" moments.

Scott brilliantly wove the "Oh, Carl!" phrase and turned it into a "Go, Carl!" exhortation as he praised the memory of his best friend.

One "Oh, Carl!" moment came during the first few months of our marriage. Carl loved practical jokes. I, on the other hand, not so much! He went through great lengths to pull off his stunts. On one day, unknown to me, Carl rigged a very elaborate system of eye hooks and monofilament fishing line to the ceiling leading into the bathroom.

He envisioned his prank to work like this: Carl knew I would get up in the middle of the night to use the bathroom, so he planned this primitive engineering system to release a basket of Styrofoam packing bubbles just as I opened the bathroom door. Being a light sleeper, I had learned to navigate the pathway to the bathroom without turning on a light and barely opening my eyes. Can you imagine how this went down when I opened the door to the bathroom and all these "white" things came down on my head? I wanted to kill him! Carl thought it was hilarious.

I am not sure what his rationale was behind all the bathroom pranks, but on yet another night during those first months of marriage, and again during my nightly bathroom visit, I went to sit down on the toilet only to hear this canned voiced saying, "I'm working down here!" Carl had purchased some prank toy and attached it to the toilet seat.

There was one more prank during this time frame. I suppose Carl felt he needed to complete a trilogy. Again on yet one more nightly bathroom run, I sat down on the seat. He had wrapped the entire toilet with clear plastic wrap. By this third episode I thought to myself. "What have I done?" "Who have I married?" This, however, was the same man who years later on Valentine's Day gave me a certified document stating a star in the galaxy had been named after me. Oh, the agony and the ecstasy of being married to Carl B Peters! There are too many practical joke stories to share in this one chapter, but allow me one more.

First a small back-story. In the 1990s, our precious friend Frances, who is also a practical jokester, sent Carl and me a beautiful greeting card and gift by mail. We read the card first. It was a lovely card thanking us for our love, friendship, and godly virtues. She signed off with a scripture from the gospel of Matthew, chapter five, verse thirty, to be exact. I'm a student of the scriptures, but do not always recognize the passage by chapter and verse. Not bothering to look up the scripture first, we proceeded straight away to open the gift. Yikes! It was a realistic rubberized right hand and arm, complete with a white-sleeved shirt and cuff, cut off at the elbow. We were startled and amused at this clever joke. The Matthew scripture? *"And if your hand, even your stronger hand, causes you to sin, cut it off and throw it away."*

189

In the fall of the same year I was preparing for my annual trip to Israel. Carl would not be accompanying me, so I traveled alone. He walked me to the gate at Tampa International, and I was on my way to Israel via one stop in New York. Even prior to 9/11 Israel has always been known for its excellent security measures for those traveling EL AL flights to Tel Aviv. It was security protocol to open each suitcase and hand check your luggage before loading it on board. There I was standing in line at JFK International waiting for my luggage to be inspected. The beautiful Israeli attendant opened my suitcase and let out a scream! Carl had somehow, at some time, without my knowledge, opened my suitcase and placed the rubberized arm, palm up, with a handwritten note that read, "I miss you already." I had to explain Carl to the EL AL representative. She looked at me and shook her head saying, "Your husband is crazy!" She had experienced an "Oh, Carl!" moment. I had to laugh to myself as I boarded. He had done it again!

This was the beginning of years trying to outdo each other "hiding" the arm. A few of the locations where we tried to achieve the element of surprise was my lingerie drawer (Carl), the hand wrapped around a roasted turkey drumstick in the oven (Yvonne), in the refrigerator vegetable drawer (Carl), and other places too numerous to mention.

Combined, we made modest salaries during our life together—always sufficient but never extravagant. He wanted to buy the children a go-cart for Christmas. I don't remember the details, but I am almost certain he had to wheel and deal with someone to afford the purchase. Instead of trying to wrap the go-cart or simply taking Zana and Robby outside on Christmas morning to show it to them, he devised an elaborate surprise. Carl loved the element of surprise and was willing to go to great lengths to achieve it.

After the children went to bed, Carl took a huge ball of string, whose ultimate resting place would be under the Christmas tree the next morning. He tied the string to the cart in the shed and circuitously created a path throughout the yard, around the house, and amongst all the trees in the yard. When the children woke up on Christmas morning the ball of sting was waiting for them. What a time they had running through the maze and winding string as they eagerly searched for the end. Carl's antics created this tension between "Oh, Carl!" and "Go, Carl!," and he kept you guessing on who you would find.

During those years in my thirties and forties, I failed to see how precious these crazy moments would be upon reflection. I enjoyed them then, I laughed then, but I didn't have the depth of emotional character to recognize magical moments. Though I engaged in the moment, I didn't savor the event for long because I was preoccupied with my next moment. Where I was going, what I was going to do, how I was going to prepare. My takeaway? Savor precious moments of joy and, yes, even stupidity! Taste it! Enjoy it! Truthfully those moments only come once. I'm okay with an "Oh, Yvonne!" these days. I'm convinced it will turn out to be a "Go, Yvonne!" in the end.

The "Oh, Carl!" years.

LOVE: THE GREATEST THING

*"Three things will last forever—faith, hope
and love—and the greatest of these is love."*
1 Corinthians 13:13

I'VE HAD AN awareness of the presence of God since childhood. And though I loved God, I must confess it was difficult believing He loved me. I accepted the intellectual understanding of Christ's sacrificial death on the cross. I gave mental assent this act was proof of His great love for me, but honestly, it was hard to receive and apply to the deepest recesses of my heart.

I have carried an insatiable desire to be loved for as long as I can remember. Please understand, it wasn't that I was not loved, but I found it difficult to receive love. Recognizing Jesus as my Savior brought tremendous healing, but I still had difficulty accepting the depths of His love for me. Ironically, experiencing widowhood was the key to receptivity. Bereavement is devastating. All your moorings are gone, and your bearings are blurred. Suddenly your personal "normal" does not exist and will never exist again. It was amid this, one of my darkest moments, that I experienced and embraced the love of God personally.

I experienced this love through small miracles of provision and care pouring in from people, beyond my immediate family, who loved Carl and me. This love came not merely with words of condolence but was manifested in action. These acts of care and kindness were expressed in practical ways from folks who mowed my lawn for months (thank you, Ron and Jan) to those who helped price numerous items for a garage sale (thank you, PT, Mar, and Rene). A realtor was sent from heaven to sell my house (thank you, Don). Countless dinner invitations were extended for holidays, special occasions, and ordinary Tuesdays (thank you, Osborne and Chamberlain families). An extraordinary lunch date turned into a special spiritual gift (thank you, Jeff and Linda). Two special friends visited nightly and ministered communion and prayer to Carl (there are not enough words to thank you, Scott and Daryse). My former dance partner, now priest, flew in from Miami to pray for Carl (thank you, Father Alejandro). Another friend drove hours to give Carl a massage (thank you, Roy). Personal artistic gifts were created for me (thank you, Debbie and Joe, Kirk and Deby). I received financial provision for incidentals from friends all over the world (you know who you are!). I was completely overwhelmed with this outpouring of love with legs. I felt utterly cherished by my heavenly Father and those He sent. He anticipated and provided for needs I was too numb to perceive. Oh, such love extended from those who themselves were loved by God.

It is difficult to comprehend the sacrificial love Jesus demonstrated at the cross. It is equally difficult to receive this love, allow it to change you, and then flow through you to others. Recently while reading 1 Corinthians 13, I glimpsed a perspective I hadn't considered. I imagined Jesus speaking to me from the cross.

> *I show my love to you by being patient and kind. I am the God of compassion and mercy. I am slow to anger and filled with unfailing love and faithfulness. That is the love I extend to you! I did not boast of being God, nor did I proudly call down angels to release me from what I came to accomplish as a sacrifice for you. I was not rude to those who despised me, who disagreed with me. In the Garden of Gethsemane, when I was struggling to the point of sweating blood, I did not demand my own way. I chose the will of My Father. I do not keep a record of*

wrongs you commit. Indeed, as far as the east is from the west, so far have I removed your transgressions. I do not rejoice with injustice, but rejoice when truth wins. I am the way, the truth, and the life. I am greater in you than any power in the world. I never give up on you. I will be with you always. I will neither fail you nor abandon you. I will never lose faith in you. For I hold you by your right hand. I, the LORD your God, say to you, do not be afraid. I am here to help you. I have given you a living hope through my resurrection. You will live and never die. My love endures in every circumstance, for I am good and my steadfast love endures forever.

Beyond the Dance is a telling of a constant and progressive surrender to this amazing redemptive love, a timeless and eternal love from the God who formed me in the womb and numbered my days. It is my testament to a God who fashioned a destiny for my life and breathed purpose into my years.

In an entry from my journal dated February 2001, I sensed the Lord speaking. *"Love is the highest law of my kingdom. The principle against which there is no other law.*

The privilege of authority rests on this law. In each situation or circumstance I bring my people into, they have a choice to love or not to love, to obey or not to obey. What they choose in each circumstance determines their level of standing and enjoyment in my presence and in my kingdom."

Have I walked perfectly in His law of love? Have I always listened to God's promptings? Waited for His timing? The answer is no! But my heart has expanded and grown more and more inclined to trust and obey this God of all Creation, this God whose essence is love, this God who desires relationship with me. The gift of dance freed my soul and birthed purpose for my life. Unconditional, forever and eternal love saved me, shaped me, and sealed me as His servant. *"For this is how God loved the world: He gave his one and only Son, so that everyone who believes in him will not perish but have eternal life."* (John 3:16)

The imagery present in "The Song of Solomon" captures the intimate love between a king and his chosen sister/lover/bride. The characters of the prose are Solomon and the Shulamite woman. The chapters are filled with verses of intimate passion, a love as strong as death, torrential waters incapable of quenching love, and meadows where lovers dance; the narrative is sweeping and quite romantic. Included as part of biblical cannon, "The Song of Solomon" is analogous to the story of the "forever" love God has for

His people. There is a King, Jesus. There is a Bride, those who set their affections on the King. The King and His Bride are set in a grand story of intimacy requiring the Bride's receptivity and openness to receive the fullness of love offered by the King, and her attentiveness to be loyally fixed on the King who offers all things. It is the greatest love story of all time.

One of the choral refrains from chapter eight is especially potent to me in this season. I prefer the translation from the "*Complete Jewish Bible*" by David H. Stern which reads, "*Who is this, coming up from the desert leaning on her darling?*"[27] My inner voice is shouting to the choir, "*Me! It's me! I'm coming out from the wilderness leaning on the arm of my Beloved!*" The wilderness season is behind me; the fruitful plain is before me.

Our pilgrimage on the earth in the scriptures is compared to a race. I am still running mine. I refuse to quit. And my hope is to finish strong. In the recent months I have found myself dancing in my kitchen while listening to my favorite eclectic picks on Pandora. The classical station brings out the ballerina in me. Gloria Estefan's songs touch my Hispanic soul, and salsa seamlessly slips out. Chris Tomlin, Hillsongs, and Bethel selections bring me to my knees. I'm dancing again!

In every season of life the Lover of my soul has quickened me to trust beyond borders, leaving behind what has been and reaching for what awaits. Good things, God things are found *Beyond the Dance.*

> *Now all glory to God, who is able, through his mighty power at work within us, to accomplish infinitely more than we might ask or think. Glory to him in the church and in Christ Jesus through all generations forever and ever! Amen.* (Ephesians 3:20–21)

WORKS CITED

1. HUFF POST, "Planting Seeds and Legacy," http://huffingtonpost.com (April 3, 2012)

2. Ravi Zacharias, *The Grand Weaver*, (USA: Zondervan, 2007), page 14

3. World Wide Words, "Once Upon a Time," http://worldwidewords.org (n.d.).

4. Then Again, "Western and Central European Chronology," http://thenagain.info (n.d.).

5. Dell F. Sanchez, Ph. D., *Aliyah! The Exodus Continues:* (USA: Authors Choice Press, 2001,2006), pages 212, 220.

6. Metro Lyrics, "Frankie Laine," http://metrolyrics.com (n.d.).

7. Wikipedia, "Rapunzel," http://en.m.wikipedia.org (n.d.).

8. Pachamama Alliance, "The Japanese Art of Kintsugi: Perfection Through Imperfection," http://pachamama.org (November 26, 2014).

9. NSC Blog, "The Monkey's Fist: An Ancient Parable for Modern Times," http://nscblog.com (November 30, 2007).

10. John Maxwell, *Intentional Living: Choosing a Life That Matters,* (USA: Center Street-Publisher, 2015), page 22.

11. Peter Wade, "Hudson Taylor," http://peterwade.com, (n.d.).

12. Julia Cameron and Mark Bryan, *The Artist's Way,* (New York: G.P. Putnam's Sons,1992), page36.

13. Julia Cameron and Mark Bryan, *The Artist's Way,* (New York: G.P. Putnam's Sons,1992) page 9.

14. Wikipedia, "Gehenna," http://en.m.wikipedia.org (n.d.).

15. A Holy Experience, "A Holy Experience," www.aholyexperience.com (January 7, 2016).

16. Tanzanite America, "Tanzanite America," www.tanzaniteamerica.com (n.d.).

17. Different Spirit, "What Gethsemane Means," http://www.differentspirit.org (n.d.).

18. Dr. Seuss, *Gerald McBoing, Boing,* (USA: Simon and Schuster Inc. and Artists and Writers Guild Inc.,1952).

19. AZQUOTES, "Tertullian," http://azquotes.com (n.d.).

20. Wikipedia, "Tudor Turtle," http://en.m.wikipedia.org (n.d.).

21. Different Spirit, "What Gethsemane Means," http://www.differentspirit.org (n.d.).

22. Merriam-Webster Online Dictionary, "Incarn," http://merriam-webster.com (n.d.).

23. Goodreads, "Fr. Craig Scott Quotes," http://goodreads.com (n.d.).

24. Got Questions, "Bible Answers for Almost All Your Questions," http://www.gotquestions.org (n.d.).

25. Dr. E. Charlotte Baker, *The Eye of the Needle,* (USA: Engeltal, 1994).

26. CRTA, "Westminster Shorter Catechism," http://reformed. org (n.d.).

27. David H. Stern, *Complete Jewish Bible,* (USA and Israel: Jewish New Testament Publications, (1998).

CPSIA information can be obtained
at www.ICGtesting.com
Printed in the USA
LVOW08s1150210717
542152LV00001B/6/P